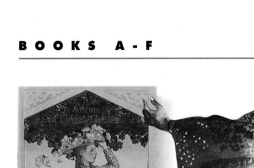

Here's all the great literature in this grade level of *Celebrate Reading!*

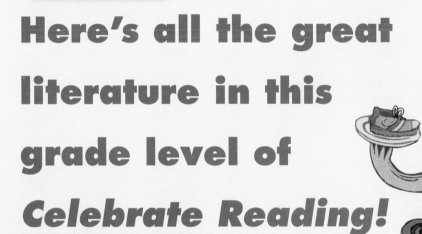

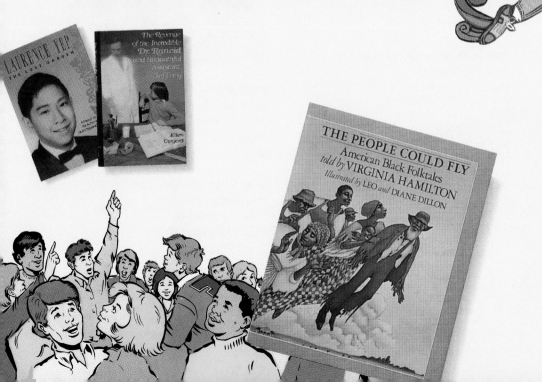

"Mom, Mom, My Ears Are Growing!"

And Other Joys of the Real World

Bingo Brown, Gypsy Lover
from the novel by
Betsy Byars
✸ *School Library Journal*
Best Book
✸ ALA Notable Children's Book

The Cybil War
from the novel by
Betsy Byars
✸ ALA Notable Children's Book
✸ Children's Choice

Remarkable Children
from the book by
Dennis Brindell Fradin

And Still I Rise
from the collection by
Maya Angelou
✸ *School Library Journal*
Best Book

**How It Feels to Fight
for Your Life**
from the book by
Jill Krementz
✸ Outstanding Science
Trade Book
✸ Teachers' Choice

**Fast Sam, Cool Clyde,
and Stuff**
from the novel by
Walter Dean Myers
✸ Children's Choice

**The Summer of
the Falcon**
from the novel by
Jean Craighead George
✸ Newbery Medal Author

Featured Poet
Maya Angelou

Look Both Ways
Seeing the Other Side

Featured Poets
Carl Sandburg
Sara Henderson Hay

Free to Fly

A User's Guide to the Imagination

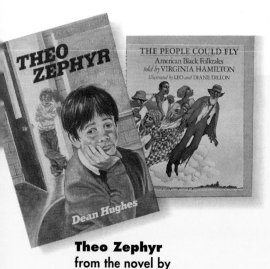

Theo Zephyr
from the novel by
Dean Hughes
✹ Children's Choice

**The People Could Fly:
American Black Folktales**
from the collection by
Virginia Hamilton
Illustrations by Leo and
Diane Dillon
✹ *New York Times* Best Illustrated
✹ ALA Notable Children's Book

**Joyful Noise: Poems
for Two Voices**
from the collection by
Paul Fleischman
✹ Newbery Medal

**The Town Cat and
Other Tales**
from the collection by
Lloyd Alexander
✹ Newbery Medal Author
✹ American Book
Award Author

**The Foundling and Other
Tales of Prydain**
from the collection by
Lloyd Alexander
✹ *School Library Journal*
Best Book

Cinderella Finds Time
by Val R. Cheatham

In Search of Cinderella
by Shel Silverstein
✹ ALA Notable Children's Book

Glass Slipper
by Jane Yolen
✹ Kerlan Award Author

**...And Then the Prince
Knelt Down and Tried
to Put the Glass Slipper
on Cinderella's Foot**
by Judith Viorst
✹ Christopher Award Author

**Yeh Shen: A Cinderella Story
from China**
retold by Ai-Ling Louie
Illustrations by Ed Young
✹ ALA Notable Children's Book

Featured Poets
Paul Fleischman
Pat Mora
Shel Silverstein
Jane Yolen
Judith Viorst

Journey Home

and Other Routes to Belonging

Featured Poets
Gwendolyn Brooks
Edwin Muir

Arriving Before I Start

Passages Through Time

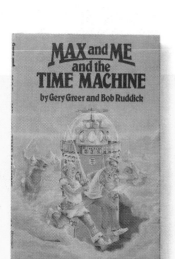

Max and Me and the Time Machine
from the novel by Gery Greer and Bob Ruddick
* *School Library Journal* Best Book

Journey to Technos
by Claire Boiko

The Day the Mountain Blew Apart
by Chris Copeland

Pompeii: Nightmare at Midday
by Kathryn Long Humphrey

Tails of the Bronx
from the collection by Jill Pinkwater

Children of the Wild West
from the book by Russell Freedman
* ALA Notable Children's Book
* Notable Social Studies Trade Book
* Teachers' Choice

Great Summer Olympic Moments
from the book by Nate Aaseng

Maya Ballplayers
by Peter Kvietok

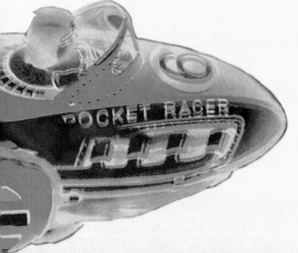

Just Like a Hero
Talk About Leadership

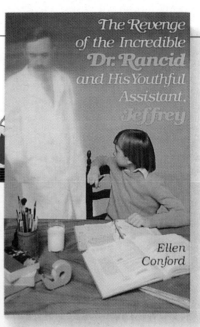

The Revenge of the Incredible Dr. Rancid and His Youthful Assistant, Jeffrey
from the novel by
Ellen Conford
✳ Young Readers' Choice Award Author

The Gold Coin
by Alma Flor Ada
✳ Christopher Award

Mother Teresa
from the biography by
Patricia Reilly Giff

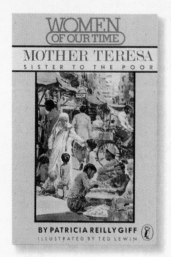

Prince of the Double Axe
by Madeleine Polland

Featured Poet
John Greenleaf Whittier

Celebrate Reading!
Trade Book Library

Our Sixth-Grade Sugar Babies
by Eve Bunting
✳ *School Library Journal* Best Book

Goodbye, Chicken Little
by Betsy Byars
✳ Children's Choice
✳ Children's Editors' Choice
✳ Library of Congress Children's Book
✳ *New York Times* Notable Book

Dragon of the Lost Sea
by Laurence Yep
✳ ALA Notable Children's Book
✳ International Reading Association 100 Favorite Paperbacks of 1989

The Westing Game
by Ellen Raskin
✳ Newbery Medal
✳ Boston Globe-Horn Book Award

The Brocaded Slipper and Other Vietnamese Tales
by Lynette Vuong

The Jedera Adventure
by Lloyd Alexander
✳ Parents' Choice

The Endless Steppe: Growing Up in Siberia
by Esther Hautzig
✳ ALA Notable Children's Book
✳ Boston Globe-Horn Book Award Honor Book
✳ Lewis Carroll Shelf Award

Baseball in April and Other Stories
by Gary Soto
✳ ALA Notable Children's Book
✳ *Parenting* Reading-Magic Award

Tom's Midnight Garden
by Philippa Pearce
✳ Carnegie Medal Winner

The House of Dies Drear
by Virginia Hamilton
✳ ALA Notable Children's Book

Journey to Jo'burg: A South African Story
by Beverly Naidoo
✳ Notable Social Studies Trade Book

Jackie Joyner-Kersee
by Neil Cohen

LOOK BOTH WAYS

Seeing the Other Side

Titles in This Set

About the Cover Artist
Guy Porfirio was born in Chicago, Illinois. He studied at the American
Academy of Art in Chicago and the School of Visual Arts in New York
City and has been an illustrator since 1980. Guy lives in Tucson, Arizona
with his wife and son.

ISBN 0-673-81167-0

1997
Scott, Foresman and Company, Glenview, Illinois
All Rights Reserved.
Printed in the United States of America.

Acknowledgments appear on page 136.

12345678910DQ010099989796

LOOK BOTH WAYS

Seeing the Other Side

ScottForesman

A Division of HarperCollins*Publishers*

Contents

Mattie

and ANGEL

from *Circle of Gold*
by Candy Dawson Boyd

Mattie curled herself into the warm center of the bed and listened for the early morning sounds of her mother and twin brother—kitchen sounds and bathroom sounds. But the apartment was silent. On the count of three, she told herself, she would get up.

One...one and a half...two...two and a half...three.... Mattie threw back the covers and jumped out of bed. When her feet touched the cold, smooth wooden floor she caught her breath and raced out of the bedroom.

A quick check of the apartment told her that Mama wasn't there. Mattie stopped to pick up the newspapers scattered on the living-room rug. Since Daddy had died, Mama had lost all interest in keeping the place neat.

Walking down the narrow hallway again, Mattie paused by her mother's room. The empty bed with its wrinkled white sheets and tossed pillows looked like a stormy sea.

Continuing down the hall, Mattie peeked into her brother's room. She could just see the top of Matt's curly head poking above the covers. His drawing pad was on the bed and the easel he used for his paintings stood against the window, draped with a sheet. The jars of water he used to wash his paintbrushes were lined up like colorful sentries along the windowsill.

In the kitchen, Mattie found a note propped against the sugar bowl on the table. *Kids, Went to work early. Will be home late. Get dinner and do your homework.*

Mattie frowned. Mama had to work late again. This was the fourth time in the past two weeks. How could Mama do the superintendent chores and work overtime at the factory too? Eventually Mrs. Rausch, the manager of their building, was going to find out that things were falling apart at 6129 Julian Street. Mrs. Adams was complaining about her dripping kitchen faucet. The Reynolds' radiators didn't work, and old Mr. Richards wanted a new stove. If word got to Rausch, Mama would be in trouble. Rausch the Rat was what Mattie called the real estate agent, but not so anyone could hear.

Mattie poured oatmeal into a pot of boiling water and stirred it furiously. She forced back the tears that came when she remembered how things used to be when Daddy was alive. He would have fixed the faucet and the radiators and ordered a new stove for Mr. Richards.

"And he would kiss me and call me his princess," Mattie murmured. Mama never did that. Mattie ached for her father. She was only eleven and it didn't seem fair that she would never see him again. Daddy had gone to work as usual one day six months ago, and on his way home some drunk driver had hit his car and killed him. From that day everything in her life had changed.

Mattie turned the stove down to simmer and called out to her brother. "Get yourself up, Matt Matisse. I've got the cereal cooking."

Matt hated oatmeal, but she couldn't stand his favorite either—Malt-o-Meal. He wouldn't be happy about the oatmeal but they had agreed that the first one up got to choose breakfast.

Mattie poured the oatmeal into two bright yellow bowls and was already eating when Matt took his place at the table. He groaned when he saw the oatmeal, but that was the only greeting he gave Mattie.

The twins ate silently, cleaned the kitchen, and left for school. Matt didn't even seem to notice the bright sunshine and cotton candy clouds that promised a glorious April day. Mattie hummed to herself as she waited for her brother to speak. When he did, the words fairly exploded out of him.

"Darn it, Mattie. Oatmeal again and I didn't have a clean shirt and I didn't have a chance to tell Mama that the Reynoldses stopped by again yesterday afternoon about their radiators. They want them fixed now," he stormed. Matt was as thin and copper-colored as Mattie, and he had the same large dark eyes.

"Look, Matt, I'll do the wash tonight. Did you tell Mr. Reynolds that Mama put in their request?"

"No, because I don't think Mama did put it in, Mattie. Things are getting worse all the time." Matt kicked at the pavement in frustration.

"Not worse, just the same," Mattie sighed. She watched her brother, knowing there was more.

"Mama won't eat," he continued. "She hardly sleeps. The house is a mess except for the times you clean it. I never know whether she's going to cry or smile or yell. We never laugh anymore, Mattie. We never have any fun. You call this a family?" His brown eyes challenged her.

Maybe it was because they were twins and twins were special, Mattie knew. But they understood one another and fiercely protected one another. Mattie wanted to say something now to comfort her brother, but before she had a chance, her best friend, Toni Douglas, called to them from the corner by her apartment building. Mattie eyed her twin and they silently agreed to erase their faces. She and Matt had always been able to communicate without using words.

"Hey, girl, ready for the math test?" Toni shouted as she waited for them to catch up. She was a bouncy, cheerful girl with bright black eyes and thick black hair that she wore in braids. A fire-engine red beret was perched on the side of her head.

"Well, are you ready?" she repeated, not even noticing when Matt barely mumbled good-bye and walked on. "I did my homework but I just know I'm going to fail. You know what, Miss Mattie Mae Benson? I'm just too young to understand fractions."

Mattie didn't answer. She pulled her thick navy sweater around her shoulders and watched Matt walk away. Her thin brown face would have been unremarkable except for her eyes. Intelligence and caution existed together in those huge brown circles. Mattie was all dark brown eyes and copper-colored angles. Not Toni Douglas. She was a chocolate bubble floating through life.

"Of course you're prepared," Toni went on, ignoring Mattie's silence. "I bet I'm the only one in class who isn't, except for those two dopes, Angel and Charlene."

Mattie groaned when she heard those names. Angel Higgley was the one person in school who gave her trouble, and Charlene was Angel's shadow. If ever anyone was misnamed, Angel Higgley was. *I wonder what she's going to try today,* Mattie thought. *I'm not going to let her copy off me. Let her start another nasty story about me, I don't care. It can't be worse than the one about me having body odor. That was mean.*

Mattie found Toni's nonstop chatter soothing. It was one of the many good things about her friend. Mattie didn't have to explain herself to Toni and answer a whole bunch of questions. They had started school together and had been friends since that first day.

"So I told Daddy," Toni was off on a new topic, "I didn't want to enter the writing contest. I mean, you know me, Mattie. English is my best subject, but I've already decided what I want to give Mom for Mother's Day. I'm going to make her a shawl. I've picked out the pattern and the yarn." Toni paused to catch her breath.

"Yeah, what does it look like?" Mattie was finally jolted into conversation.

"The yarn is lavender with silver threads running through it. I saw it at Stern's. The pattern is really fancy, but Mrs. Stamps said she'd help me with it. I have the money saved up. Don't you think Mom will like that?" This time Toni waited for Mattie's answer.

"She'll love it. You know how excited she gets over anything you make. Remember those funny-looking pot holders you made for her when we were in second grade?"

They laughed together as they remembered the crazy pot holders Toni had made out of purple cotton loops.

"What's the contest you were talking about?" Mattie asked.

"The one in the *South Side Daily*. Didn't you see it? You have to write an essay about what your mother means to you. If you win, your family gets a dinner 'in one of Chicago's better restaurants' " — Toni repeated the words in the newspaper article— "and 'movie tickets and a copy of *Roots*' too."

"No money?" Mattie asked.

"Oh, sure. First prize is fifty dollars. Not bad, huh?" Toni came to a sudden stop and grabbed Mattie's arm. "Look, Mattie. He's there."

"Who?" Mattie followed Toni's gaze.

"The new boy, the one who transferred from Ridley School. He sits right across from you. How could you ignore Larry Saunders? He's the best-looking boy in our class." Toni tugged at her braids and adjusted her beret. "Now don't act like you see him or like we've been talking about him," Toni warned.

Mattie smiled at her friend. Toni was practically dancing with anticipation. The girls had to cross the corner where Larry was stationed as a crossing guard this morning.

"If we work it just right," Toni said, "we can get held up by the light. That will give us thirty-seven seconds. Miracles can happen in thirty-seven seconds. Maybe he'll speak to us." Toni clenched her teeth to stop from grinning. "How do I look?" she asked.

"On a scale of one to ten, maybe a three," Mattie teased.

"Oh, no. What's wrong with me? Tell me."

"Nothing's wrong with you. You look fine. I was just teasing. You look better than Angel Higgley."

"Now you are making fun of me." Toni pulled at one of her braids. "She's the best-dressed girl in class."

"No, I'm not making fun of you. You're better than Angel any day and anyone with good sense can see that," Mattie declared.

"I hope Larry can see it," Toni said, taking Mattie's arm and heading for the corner.

But when they got to the intersection, Larry was so busy urging a line of straggling children across the street that he just looked back and waved the two girls across.

"Come on," Larry yelled. "Hurry up!"

"Toni, I'm crossing with or without you," Mattie said.

Toni was forced to move. This wasn't the way she had planned it. She ran across the street, catching up with Mattie as she stepped up on the opposite curb.

"You two are worse than the little kids." Larry glared at them.

Without a word, the two friends hurried away. Toni yanked her beret off and stuffed it in her pocket.

"Who does he think he is?" she sputtered, looking back over her shoulder.

"The best-looking boy in class." Mattie grinned at her friend, and they both broke out in laughter and raced to the school building.

The bell hadn't rung for class yet so the girls leaned into the chain-link fence that surrounded the playground and watched their schoolmates. The concrete pounded with the sounds of double-dutch. At least a dozen pairs of feet hit the pavement in a steady rhythm. Mattie chanted the rope song as she and Toni watched their classmates dash in and out of the swiftly turning ropes.

Sally Sue went to school early Monday morning.
Sally Sue went to school early Monday morning.
Double-down, double-down, double-down,
Sally Sue.
Double-down, double-down, double-down,
Sally Sue.

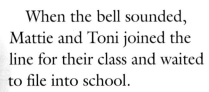

When the bell sounded, Mattie and Toni joined the line for their class and waited to file into school.

"So here's the math whiz, Mattie Mae Benson." The voice of Angel Higgley came from somewhere behind Mattie in line. "Bet she's going to get a hundred on the test today. What do you think, Charlene?"

Mattie hunched her shoulders defensively as the taunting words curled around her. She was grateful when the line began to move.

"You bet she is," Toni shouted. "She's going to get another hundred and she's going to sing about it all the way home." Toni knew she had scored. All the kids remembered that Angel had tried out for the lead in the school musical last year and lost to Mattie.

"You've got some things to worry about, Toni Douglas," Angel threatened. "If you don't watch out you're going to lose that funny-look-ing hat of yours. Too bad you can't lose some of that blubber as easily."

As Angel pushed ahead of her into the class-room, Toni grabbed at the hat that was working its way out of her pocket.

Mattie stared at Angel's sleek page-boy. There wasn't a hair out of place. Mattie yearned to mess it up, twist it until Angel begged for mercy. One rough twist for every cruel word. But her father had told her that fighting was the easy way out. "Stay cool," he had said.

Mattie put her arm around Toni's shoulders. "Don't let her get to you. Angel's the one with blubber."

"Yeah. Where? I don't see it."

"She's got blubber on the brain." Mattie laughed. "See you at recess." She hugged Toni and hurried over to the cluster of desks she shared with Michael, Larry, Charlene, and Angel. When the math test was passed out Mattie set to work. Daddy was right. If you stayed cool you made it through.

Mattie finished the test before anyone else and turned her paper over on her desk. She reached inside for a book. Out of the corner of her eye she caught Angel's catlike gaze. Her eyes were moving back and forth from her test paper to Mattie's. The meaning was clear.

Mattie jerked her chair back and picked up her paper. Mr. Ashby, her teacher, was monitoring the class from the back of the room. Mattie headed straight for him. Putting the paper into his hands, she reached for the bathroom pass. Mr. Ashby nodded permission.

There was no telling what Angel would do to her for this, but Mattie didn't care. Not too many kids dared to cross Miss Queen Bee. Mattie was angry with the bunch of dopes who always hung around Angel. Girls who wished their eyes were gray instead of black. Girls who dreamed of having long wavy hair like the white girls on television. Girls who didn't realize that they, too, were lovely and special.

When she got back to her classroom, Mr. Ashby was collecting the test papers. Mattie slid into her chair avoiding Angel's eyes. A piece of paper was sticking out of her desk. She reached for it in anticipation, expecting one of Toni's funny messages. But the note wasn't on the bright green paper Toni used.

Mattie sensed trouble. Charlene was watching her over the top of her speller. Unfolding the note carefully in her lap, Mattie read the words: *Trouble is coming your way.* The white notepaper had a skull and crossbones sticker on it.

Without looking up Mattie pushed the note deep into her desk. Angel was getting even. Should she give the note to Mr. Ashby? The very thought set her heart pounding. She couldn't be a

tattletale. Anyway, she had no real proof. It was her word against Angel's. Mattie's stomach knotted. She wasn't a fighter in Angel's league.

So, what are you going to do about Angel?" Toni asked.

Recess had just started and Toni and Mattie were walking along beside the fence of the playground, as far from Angel and her crowd as they could get.

"I should go to Mr. Ashby and say—"

"Yeah, say what?" Toni interrupted. "Mr. Ashby, I found this note in my desk, and I know Angel wrote it because I wouldn't let her copy the answers on my math test?"

"That's what I should say," Mattie muttered.

"And what do you think he would say?" Toni demanded. " 'Angel Higgley, I've had enough of your sneaky ways. You are going to the principal's office'?"

"Maybe," Mattie murmured.

"Mattie Mae Benson, you're a dreamer. That's not going to happen. Angel is too smart to get caught. You don't have any real proof. You think that robot, Charlene, is going to tell on her?"

"Well, what am I supposed to do? Turn into a bully like her?"

"You could tell your mother or Matt."

"No, Mama's too upset already. And what could Matt do? I don't want to get him into trouble. No, I can't let them know about this, and don't you say a word. Promise?"

"Okay. Okay. Cross my heart and hope to pass the next math test." Toni grinned.

Mattie stared through the fence at the park across the street. The trees were covered with new green leaves, and fresh spring grass spread over the ground like a rich carpet.

"What are you thinking about?" Toni leaned back against the fence.

"That park is special to me. There are all kinds of trees there—one called the gingko tree from Asia. The leaves are shaped like small green fans. There's only one in the whole park. My father and I found it—I can remember the day.

"Daddy had just come home from work and I was reading a book about Dr. King. I couldn't understand why black people weren't allowed to vote and had to sit in the back of the buses. Daddy took me to the park to talk about it. He didn't even change his clothes before we went— funny what you remember. We found the tree and later I went to the library and found out what it was. Daddy called it our fan tree. It was our special tree." Mattie's eyes filled with tears.

"Don't cry, Mattie. I'll stick by you, and I won't let Angel bother you either."

The rest of the morning passed uneventfully. At noon Mattie and Toni shared their lunches. On their way back to their classroom, Mattie saw a new, colorful bulletin board display in the hall. It had Matt's artistic stamp all over it.

"Toni, look! Another Matt special."

"He's good all right," Toni agreed. "Your mother must be proud of him."

"I wish she was proud of me. She finds fault with everything I do. Everything!"

"She's just not herself, with your father gone and all. It's not you, Mattie, really. Come on, we have to go. The bell's ringing."

All afternoon Mattie waited, tense and expectant, for Angel to carry out her threat. But nothing happened. When it was time to go home, Mattie gathered her books together. She had to carry all of them home because Mr. Ashby believed in giving homework assignments. As she walked over to get in line to leave, Toni called to her.

"I have to talk to Mr. Ashby about the math test. Wait for me outside."

Mattie left the room and started down the steps, clutching the load of books in both arms. She was helpless when it happened. Someone pushed her—hard. Startled, she let the books fly and grabbed the rail to break her fall. Stunned, she searched the faces around her.

There weren't any teachers or monitors in sight.

Mattie looked up into Charlene's wide eyes. She seemed frightened as she thrust a library book into Mattie's hands. "You sure are clumsy, Mattie Benson. Maybe she needs some lessons in walking. Huh, Angel?"

Pulling on her bangs, Angel stared at Mattie. "Or maybe she doesn't understand about notes with skulls and crossbones on them," Angel said.

"You lay one hand on me—you push me again, and I'm going to get you—both of you," Mattie shouted.

"And I'll be right there to back her up." Toni had appeared at the top of the stairs. "Come on, if you two want a fight, let's go."

As Toni started down the stairs, the two bullies ran off, screaming with laughter.

"Mattie, what happened?" Toni asked.

"I was going down the stairs and one of them pushed me."

"Have you got all your stuff?" Toni asked, picking up a stray sheet of notebook paper.

"I guess so. Hey, what got into us? We actually sounded like we were going to fight them. What if they'd taken us up on it?" Mattie giggled.

"I was so mad! We do have our limits though, Mattie. Enough is enough," Toni declared as they left the school building.

"Toni, I've got to hurry. I have to go home and then go to the Bacons to baby-sit. What are you doing tomorrow?"

"I want to go downtown and get the yarn for Mom's present. Why don't you come? We haven't done anything fun on a Saturday in a long time. Let's go together."

"I don't know what Mama will say. I have all this homework to do."

"Mattie, even condemned prisoners feast one last time. We deserve a break. We stood up to the two ghouls. Come on, we'll just be gone part of the day." Toni knew by the slow grin on Mattie's face that she had won.

"Let me clear it with Mama. I'll call you in the morning. By nine," Mattie said, as she ran off up the street.

BEHIND
CIRCLE OF GOLD

Changes and Choices
by Candy Dawson Boyd

I never wanted to become an author. My childhood dreams glittered like the slinky dresses I fantasized about wearing in nightclubs, singing like Sarah Vaughn. Sometimes I saw myself acting on the stage, confident and talented. Such dramatic dreams for an African American girl growing up on the Southside of Chicago! Little did I know that my life would veer away from fancy dresses, sad songs, and the drama of the theater. I had no idea that I was headed for libraries, public schools, author talks, and colleges.

My parents believed in education and the importance of being a reading thinker. Every Saturday I hurried to the small public library on 61st Street. I read hundreds of books. But I seldom saw my face in any of them. Worse, I never relived my family life or that of our neighbors in those books. Questions filled my head. Where were stories about African American families? Weren't there African American children who worried about passing tests,

making the team, parents divorcing, being liked? Didn't we dream? Didn't our parents dream for us and labor for those dreams? Where was my Daddy? Why was I invisible in the world of children's literature?

When I moved to Berkeley, California, the books, questions, and experiences of my life formed a crude circle. In my fifth-grade classroom I taught a rainbow of children from many ethnic groups. Searching stacks of books for young people in libraries brought back the old questions. Where were my children? Why weren't their lives in books?

So I decided to write books for children. Over a period of two years I read every children's book in the public library. I took two university courses in writing for young people. With the help of one of my teachers, I mailed manuscripts to publishers. For nine years I received rejection letters and returned manuscripts. Finally, I gave up. I shoved the manuscripts out of sight and sobbed. Candy Dawson Boyd was a stupid, dumb failure.

After a while, feeling sorry for myself got boring. I decided to write an "ordinary" story about a girl named Mattie who needs to win her mother's love. Mattie would live in Chicago and would love to read, just like I had. She would have a twin brother. I thought that might add an interesting twist. I remembered a best friend I once had and gave her to Mattie in the character of Toni.

Mattie wasn't enough of a name. I wanted her name to flow. Mattie Mae Benson sounded good. Her father was dead. My father did not die, but my parents divorced when I was young. The mother would be upset, trying to deal with the death of her husband and providing for two children. My mama struggled to raise three children. I drew upon my life like a deep well full of questions. What happened to Mattie would be the story I wanted to write. Once I knew my characters' full names, I knew who they were and what they might do. I had a book.

Where did these ideas go? I pencilled them into a notepad. Then I set up a notebook with tabs for title, characters, plot, problem, background, situation, and research. Over the weeks that followed I described the characters first, then completed each section of the notebook. Then I sat down at a computer to write. Ideas popped into my head when I was teaching, washing clothes, driving, sitting in a movie, or brushing my teeth. I'd jot them down. I didn't have a regular schedule to write. Working full-time and going to school meant that I wrote whenever I could.

I read each chapter aloud, listening for a sense of rhythm, coherence, and my sound. Using pencils, I'd make changes, scribbling all over the pages, reading them aloud over and over until it sounded "right." Finally, I had a collection of chapters that told a story about a girl I loved and the problems she faced. I had a manuscript. After two publishers rejected my manuscript, a third one accepted it. I was an author! Mattie Mae Benson, her mother, her brother, Toni, Mr. Ashby, Angel, and Charlene waited in the pages of a book for someone to open and enjoy. No longer were the memories and dreams they stood for invisible.

Every one of my books begins in a small pad as a series of somewhat connected ideas. Then IF those ideas begin to cluster together and form a story that excites me, captures my curiosity, and begins to move on its own—I celebrate! I have a book! For me books don't come easily nor does time to write. However, I got concerned about the paucity of ordinary stories about African Americans. Out of that came *Circle of Gold*. The need to honor children's complex lives resulted in a sequel to *Circle of Gold* entitled *Breadsticks and Blessing Places,* in which Toni needs Mattie's help when a tragedy occurs. Unresolved questions about how World War II affected my father caused me to think about the right of children to speak out about this world. Meshing that with my experiences during the Vietnam War allowed me to write *Charlie Pippin*. Now I am concerned about something else, and out of that will come a book. Where will this book take me? What will I learn? What problems will I need to solve? Who and what, once invisible, will be seen in strong, clear light?

Some people wonder why a college professor writes books for young people. The answer is simple. I must. When I write, I know that there is a chance that we can understand one another a bit more. Each story opens new doors, allowing me to enter the lives of children and forge a glowing Circle of Gold.

Thinking About It

1 As you read this story, what did you want Mattie to do? What did you want her to say?

2 What did Mattie ever do to get Angel and Charlene upset with her? Could Mattie do something so they would stop bothering her? If so, what would it be? Should she do it?

3 Suppose you want to show Mattie as she really *is*—not the way she looks, but her true self. How would you do it? What would be the result?

Another Book by Candy Dawson Boyd

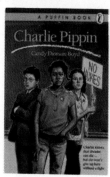

In *Charlie Pippin,* an eleven-year-old girl is determined to learn about the Vietnam War so that she can understand her father, who fought in it.

PEER MEDIATION

by Priscilla Prutzman and
Judith M. Johnson

It may not have been the worst crash in the 9:30 A.M. between-class break, but everyone agreed it was *one* of the worst.

Here's what happened. Josh Hunter, on the run, was sorting through his notebook trying to find out how many diameters it takes to make a circumference. The loose-leaf rings were open and about ninety-seven pages of math notes were hanging there, like leaves before a storm. Herb Presidio was on the floor tying his sneaker. At the same time, he was trying to balance the pieces of his science project so that he could carry it to class. It was a weather barometer consisting of a jar with rubber stretched across the top, a very delicate balsa indicator, and a gauge.

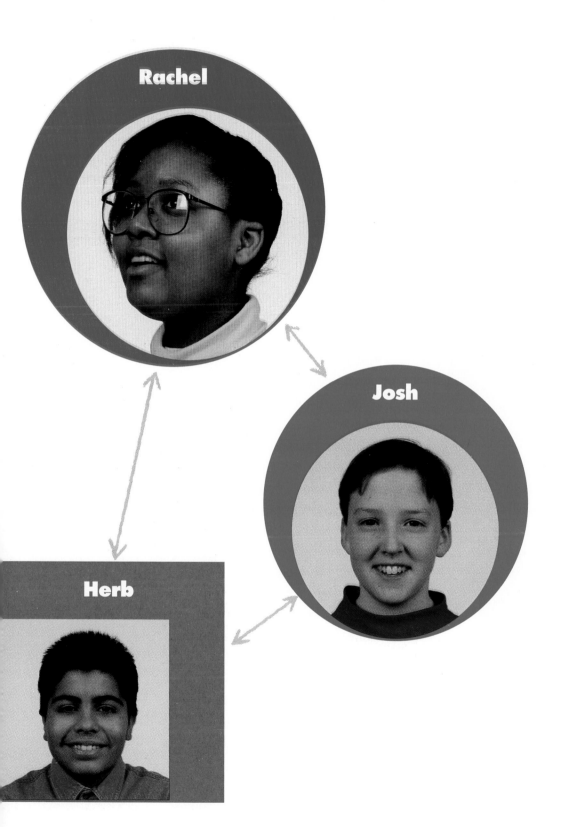

Rachel

Josh

Herb

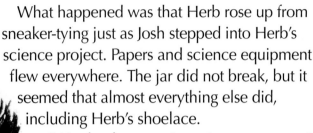

What happened was that Herb rose up from sneaker-tying just as Josh stepped into Herb's science project. Papers and science equipment flew everywhere. The jar did not break, but it seemed that almost everything else did, including Herb's shoelace.

"Watch where you're going, you twerp," shouted Herb. The warning bell sounded. Josh said nothing. He just scooped up fallen papers and scurried. "You smashed my barometer!" Herb shouted after him. "I'll get you for this!"

In Room 201D Josh Hunter crammed his papers into the notebook, forced it shut, and slid it into the portal under his desk.

"That's right. Clear your desks. You'll need nothing but a pencil," said Mr. Prescott. "The geometry quiz will take exactly twenty minutes. Then we'll go over your homework in class."

Homework! Josh had a feeling that his homework had vanished. It must have floated away during the aftermath of the crash in the hall. Aftermath indeed! On-the-way-to-math was more like it.

Cindy tapped Josh on the shoulder just as he bent down to see if the homework might magically appear. "Are you in trouble! Herb Presidio told someone he's going to wait for you at noon hour and beat you up for destroying his science project."

"I didn't mean to," said Josh from halfway under his desk. "It was an accident. I was studying for this test."

"No more talking," said Mr. Prescott.

In room 217A Herb Presidio tried to explain his broken science project.

"One of the things we have to learn is how to take care of equipment," said Ms. Sowers. "It doesn't matter that we built our instruments for the weather unit out of 'found' materials. Even with inexpensive equipment, we cannot be careless and still be scientists. The principle is still the same."

"Yeah, the *principal* is still the same," thought Herb. "And I'm going to end up in the principal's office again." He grew angrier by the minute.

"Josh looked mad when he ran by me in the hall," Henrietta remarked. (She sat right beside Herb.) "Tracy said she heard him say something like the next time you trip him in the hall he's going to kick in your locker."

"What are you two guys going to do when you meet in the all-purpose room at noon hour?" asked Arnold Safer. He was the best student in the science class, and he always looked as if he were conducting an experiment. "Whatever it is, could you wait until I go home and get my video camera?"

"Very funny," murmured Herb. "I think it's time someone learned not to push me around."

"Or fall over you," added Henrietta. "I wonder if Josh does those things on purpose. You two better talk things over. That's what my mom would say."

What will happen? What would happen in your school? What would happen in most schools? A fight? Don't be too sure. Young people aren't all fighters. They're learning fast how to work out conflicts like this one.

That's not to say that a let's-be-buddies ending is a sure thing. Josh and Herb may not laugh, shake hands, and help each other make a new science project and redo math homework. To expect a rosy ending may be over-optimistic, like expecting a solid gold chain in your next box of Breakfast Bitties. Yet, in many schools, there's help. It is called *peer mediation. Peer* means "your own age or status." If a peer helps Josh and Herb, it won't be an adult. It will be another student their own age. *Mediation* means "giving help." Mediation does not mean that someone tells Josh and Herb what to do. *Peer mediators* aren't law-makers. They don't even say, "If I were you, here's what I would do."

What *does* happen in peer mediation? Something like this . . .

Steps in Peer Mediation

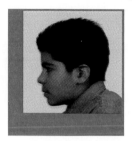
The first step is to agree to peer mediation and find a quiet place where mediation can take place. In Josh and Herb's case, it won't be the crowded all-purpose room at noon hour. One or two students, who have been appointed peer mediators, will meet Josh and Herb and take them to a quiet place. They'll sit between Josh and Herb, who are now called the *disputants*. (Disputants are people involved in a dispute, or conflict.) They'll assure Josh and Herb that they, the peer mediators, are *neutral*; that is, they will not take sides.

The second step is to lay down rules. These are not rules of good behavior, but of mediation. Here are the rules:

1. Agree to try to solve the problem.

2. Agree not to interrupt the other person.

3. Agree not to put down the other person.

4. Agree that everything said in the room is confidential.

The third step, now that there are rules to allow mediation, is that each disputant tells his or her version of the conflict. Josh tells what happened from his perspective. Herb tells what happened as he understands it. The peer mediators listen. Sometimes they ask questions or restate what a disputant has said. They ask questions or restate in order to understand. They remain neutral.

The fourth step is up to the mediators. They must help Herb and Josh stop thinking about what *has* happened and help them think now about what *may* happen next. To make this shift, the mediators ask questions such as:

1 What do you really want to happen?

2 What might happen if you don't reach an agreement?

3 What do you have in common?

Then the mediators may say, "Here's what you have to gain by solving the problem." Herb and Josh may be more willing to settle their dispute when they see how they'll benefit.

The fifth step is to look for solutions. The peer mediators ask questions such as, "What could you have done differently?" or "What could you do right now?" This step can be a brainstorming one; that is, the disputants can suggest as many possible solutions as their brains can think of, without making fun, without anyone saying, "That's a stupid idea!"

Step six: The disputants and the mediators go over the list of possible solutions. The mediators say to the disputants, "Which of these options are you willing to do?" Of course, they're looking for a win-win solution, although anyone who has seen an open notebook collide with a science project knows that such a solution has to be watered down a bit.

Step seven: Agree on a solution. Write it down. The mediators write down what each disputant agrees to do. Then everyone signs the agreement. Shake hands. The agreement is sealed!

Would you be a peer mediator?
Peer mediators must be caring, creative, and trustworthy. They have usually received at least two days of training in how to communicate, listen actively, find common ground, stay neutral, and write the agreements. Mediators are also trained to help students who aren't sure whether they want to try mediation or not. To such students, they say, "Would you like to try mediation to help you work out a solution to this problem?"

Mediators also learn to deal with students who make up fake conflicts. Sometimes students pretend that they are having a conflict in order to draw attention to themselves. Mediators learn to tell the difference between a real conflict and a fake dispute.

Some people feel that a whole school benefits when there's a peer mediation program. It is, after all, no more nor less than trying to solve conflict creatively.

What Finally Happened

Here, in play form, is how the conflict between Josh and Herb turned out. In this case, the mediator is Rachel, who finds the two boys in the all-purpose room at noon hour. They are facing each other, and Herb looks the angrier of the two.

Rachel: Herb, what are you going to do?

Herb: I'm ready to fight him. He ruined my science project and he didn't even stop to apologize or help pick up the pieces. Then he spread rumors about me.

Rachel: If you fight him, your parents will ground you or you'll end up in the principal's office— you know that. Are you and Josh willing to try mediation instead? The two of you can sit across from each other and solve this problem yourselves. I'll help.

Herb: Right now, I'm so mad at him, I couldn't even talk to him.

Rachel: Why don't you both come to our mediation center after school, after you've cooled off? *(Josh is right there listening to this.)*

Herb: Fine. Just keep me away from him now.

That afternoon Herb and Josh sit at the mediation table, with Rachel between them.

Rachel: Okay. Josh and Herb, before we start, I need to ask you to agree on some ground rules. I will remain neutral and will not take sides. Everything said in this room stays in this room. You will each get a chance to speak, uninterrupted. You will not put each other down. You agree to solve the problem. Those are the rules. Do you agree to them?

Herb: I'll try if he will.

Josh: Yeah, sure.

Rachel: Good. Now, Josh, you tell what happened.

Josh: I was walking to math class and trying to get my papers together because there was a test. I guess I figured the hallway was clear. And all of a sudden I fell over Herb and all his stuff. He seemed to be there just to block my way and get me in trouble. He yelled at me and called me a name, and it was his fault.

Rachel: So you ran into Herb and his things, and you spilled your notebook.

Josh: Right, and he didn't do anything but yell at me. And then someone told me he said he'd beat me up.

Rachel: All right. Can *you* tell what happened, Herb?

Herb: I didn't do anything. I was tying my shoe. I had my science project there, and I was trying to put it together so I could take it into class. And all of a sudden Josh jumped on me and kicked things all over.

Josh: That's not true. I didn't even realize I bumped into him. I just thought about my math papers.

Rachel: Josh, you promised not to interrupt.

Josh: Sorry.

Rachel: Go on, Herb.

Herb: Like I was saying, he didn't stop to help or anything. He just went on. I think it was on purpose, and the reason I know that is what somebody told me afterward—that he said he'd kick in my locker.

Josh: That's a lie. I never said that. You made it up.

Rachel: Now, don't forget the ground rule: You are not to put each other down. Let's go on, so we get the whole story.

Josh: Well, things were so upset that I lost my homework and I may have flunked the math test.

Herb: And I lost my science project. I mean, it didn't get any credit, and I'm already in trouble in that class.

Rachel: So each of you lost something. Each of you thinks it is the other person's fault. And each of you heard rumors that the other was going to get even. Do you have anything to add, or do we have the whole story? *(silence)* Now let's try to decide what to do next. Were you friends before this happened?

Herb: No. Well—sort of. I mean, we weren't enemies.

Josh: I wanted to be friends. I wouldn't have done anything *not* to be friends.

Rachel: Do you want to be friends now?

Herb: Maybe. I'd try if he would.

Josh: Yes.

Rachel: What else do you want to happen from this mediation?

Herb: I want an apology.

Josh: I want my homework back, and I want all the rumors to stop.

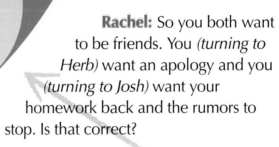

Rachel: So you both want to be friends. You *(turning to Herb)* want an apology and you *(turning to Josh)* want your homework back and the rumors to stop. Is that correct?

Herb and Josh: Yes.

Rachel: What can you do to solve this? Josh?

Josh: I could apologize. I could also promise to look where I'm going from now on.

Rachel: What about you, Herb?

Herb: I could be his friend if he apologizes to me. I could also tell some of those kids to stop telling everyone there's going to be a fight.

Rachel: Anything else?

Josh: What about my homework?

Rachel: Well, what could you do?

Herb: I could explain to Mr. Prescott what happened, and maybe he'd give you an extra day to turn it in. Maybe he'd understand if you didn't do the test right.

Josh: I really doubt it!

Herb: Well, at least *I'm* trying.

Rachel: Hey—no put-downs! I thought we were getting somewhere with this. I wrote down all the possible solutions you mentioned. Let's look them over.

(They read the list.)

Rachel: Josh, which of these things are you willing to do?

Josh: I'll apologize. I'll be more careful. I'll help tell people to stop spreading rumors. I'll tell them that Herb and I are not going to have a fight.

Rachel: So, Herb, you agree to be a friend and to talk to Mr. Prescott to help Josh. Josh, you agree to apologize and to help stop the rumors. Is there anything else?

Josh: Yes. I think I could tell Ms. Sowers what happened to Herb's science project. *(grins)* I'll tell her I wrecked it by mistake.

Herb: Would you do that? What will she say this time?

Josh: I don't know, but it's worth a try.

Rachel: *(writing)* I think I have all this down. I'll go over it and I'll have you two go over it, and when I have it right, I'll ask you to sign the form— and I'll sign it, too. Do you agree?

Josh and **Herb:** Yes

Herb: It's worth a try anyway. It could have been a lot worse.

Rachel: Congratulations! You completed the mediation successfully. I'm glad you decided to work it out.

Josh: I'm sorry about knocking your stuff over.

Herb: I'm sorry you lost your homework. I guess I did yell, and maybe that helped start the rumors.

Josh: After this, we'll ask each other. We won't believe the rumors.

Rachel: Before you go, shake hands.

(Josh and Herb shake hands to seal the agreement.)

Rachel: Thank you for letting me help you solve your dispute.

Herb: Just one thing—where am I going to get one new shoestring?

Thinking About It

1 Have you been in situations where peer mediation would have helped? How might the situation have been different if peer mediators had become involved?

2 Why is peer mediation effective? What drawbacks does it have? How could the procedure be improved?

3 You are a trained peer mediator and come up to Mattie Mae Benson and Angel Higgley just as Charlene pushes Mattie on the stairway. What do you do?

A Book About Peer Mediation

In *Sticks and Stones and Skeleton Bones,* by Jamie Gilson, the friendship of best-friends Hobie Hanson and Nick Rossi is threatened by a misunderstanding. Can it even be saved by the mediators in their classroom?

Primer Lesson

by Carl Sandburg

Look out how you use proud words.

When you let proud words go, it is

    not easy to call them back.

They wear long boots, hard boots; they

    walk off proud; they can't hear you

    calling—

Look out how you use proud words.

they walk off proud

A Tempest in the School Teapot

**from *Anne of Green Gables*
by L. M. Montgomery**

*Anne Shirley is an eleven-year-old orphan who has
just come to live with Matthew and Marilla Cuthbert
on Canada's Prince Edward Island. Like many
children in the 1800s, Anne will attend a one-room
schoolhouse.*

The Avonlea school was a whitewashed building, low in the eaves and wide in the windows, furnished inside with comfortable, substantial, old-fashioned desks that opened and shut, and were carved all over their lids with the initials and hieroglyphics of three generations of school children. The schoolhouse was set back from the road and behind it was a dusky fir wood and a brook where all the children put their bottles of milk in the morning to keep cool and sweet until dinner hour.

Marilla had seen Anne start off to school on the first day of September with many secret misgivings. Anne was such an odd girl. How would she get on with the other children? And how on earth would she ever manage to hold her tongue during school hours?

Things went better than Marilla feared, however. Anne came home that evening in high spirits.

"I think I'm going to like school here," she announced. "I don't think much of the master, though. He's all the time curling his mustache and making eyes at Prissy Andrews. Prissy is grown up, you know. She's sixteen and she's studying for the entrance examination into Queen's Academy at Charlottetown next year. Tillie Boulter says the master is *dead gone* on her. She's got a beautiful complexion and curly brown hair and she does it up so elegantly. She sits in the long seat at the back and he sits there, too, most of the time—to explain

her lessons, he says. But Ruby Gillis says she saw him writing something on her slate and when Prissy read it she blushed as red as a beet and giggled; and Ruby Gillis says she doesn't believe it had anything to do with the lesson."

"Anne Shirley, don't let me hear you talking about your teacher in that way again," said Marilla sharply. "You don't go to school to criticize the master. I guess he can teach *you* something, and it's your business to learn. And I want you to understand right off that you are not to come home telling tales about him. That is something I won't encourage. I hope you were a good girl."

"Indeed I was," said Anne comfortably. "It wasn't so hard as you might imagine, either. I sit with Diana. Our seat is right by the window and we can look down to the Lake of Shining Waters. There are a lot of nice girls in school and we had scrumptious fun playing at dinnertime. It's so nice to have a lot of little girls to play with. But of course I like Diana best and always will. I *adore* Diana. I'm dreadfully far behind the others. They're all in the fifth book and I'm only in the fourth. I feel that it's kind of a disgrace. But there's not one of them has such an imagination as I have and I soon found that out. We had reading and geography and Canadian history and dictation today. Mr. Phillips said my spelling was disgraceful and he held up my slate so that everybody could see it, all marked over. I felt so mortified, Marilla; he might have been politer to a stranger, I think. Ruby Gillis gave me an apple and Sophia Sloane lent me a lovely pink card with 'May I see you home?' on it. I'm to give it back to her tomorrow. And Tillie Boulter let me wear her bead ring all the afternoon. Can I have some of those pearl beads off the old pincushion in the garret to make myself a ring? And oh, Marilla, Jane Andrews told me that Minnie MacPherson told her that she heard Prissy Andrews tell Sara Gillis that I had a very pretty nose. Marilla, that is the first compliment I have ever had in my life and you can't imagine what a strange feeling it gave me. Marilla, have I really a pretty nose? I know you'll tell me the truth."

"Your nose is well enough," said Marilla shortly. Secretly she thought Anne's nose was a remarkable pretty one; but she had no intention of telling her so.

That was three weeks ago and all had gone smoothly so far. And now, this crisp September morning, Anne and Diana were tripping blithely down the Birch Path, two of the happiest little girls in Avonlea.

"I guess Gilbert Blythe will be in school today," said Diana. "He's been visiting his cousins over in New Brunswick all summer and he only came home Saturday night. He's *aw'fly* handsome, Anne. And he teases the girls something terrible. He just torments our lives out."

Diana's voice indicated that she rather liked having her life tormented out than not.

"Gilbert Blythe?" said Anne. "Isn't it his name that's written up on the porch wall with Julia Bell's and a big 'Take Notice' over them?"

"Yes," said Diana, tossing her head, "but I'm sure he doesn't like Julia Bell so very much. I've heard him say he studied the multiplication table by her freckles."

"Oh, don't speak about freckles to me," implored Anne. "It isn't delicate when I've got so many. But I do think that writing take-notices up on the wall about the boys and girls is the silliest ever. I should just like to see anybody dare to write my name up with a boy's. Not, of course," she hastened to add, "that anybody would."

Anne sighed. She didn't want her name written up. But it was a little humiliating to know that there was no danger of it.

"Nonsense," said Diana, whose black eyes and glossy tresses had played such havoc with the hearts of Avonlea schoolboys that her name figured on the porch walls in half a dozen take-notices. "It's only meant as a joke. And don't you be too sure your name won't ever be written up. Charlie Sloane is *dead gone* on you. He told his mother—his mother, mind you— that you were the smartest girl in school. That's better than being good looking."

"No, it isn't," said Anne, feminine to the core. "I'd rather be pretty than clever. And I hate Charlie Sloane, I can't bear a boy with goggle eyes. If anyone wrote my name up with his I'd *never* get over it, Diana Barry. But it *is* nice to keep head of your class."

"You'll have Gilbert in your class after this," said Diana, "and he's used to being head of his class, I can tell you. He's only in the fourth book although he's nearly fourteen. Four years ago his father was sick and had to go out to Alberta for his health and Gilbert went with him. They were there three years and Gil didn't go to school hardly any until they came back. You won't find it so easy to keep head after this, Anne."

"I'm glad," said Anne quickly. "I couldn't really feel proud of keeping head of little boys and girls of just nine or ten. I got up yesterday spelling 'ebullition.' Josie Pye was head and, mind you, she peeped in her book. Mr. Phillips didn't see her—he was looking at Prissy Andrews—but I did. I just swept her a look of freezing scorn and she got as red as a beet and spelled it wrong after all."

"Those Pye girls are cheats all round," said Diana indignantly, as they climbed the fence of the main road. "Gertie Pye actually went and put her milk bottle in my place in the brook yesterday. Did you ever? I don't speak to her now."

When Mr. Phillips was in the back of the room hearing Prissy Andrews's Latin, Diana whispered to Anne, "That's Gilbert Blythe sitting right across the aisle from you, Anne. Just look at him and see if you don't think he's handsome."

Anne looked accordingly. She had a good chance to do so, for the said Gilbert Blythe was absorbed in stealthily pinning the long yellow braid of Ruby Gillis, who sat in front of him, to the back of her seat. He was a tall boy, with curly brown hair, roguish hazel eyes, and a mouth twisted into a teasing smile. Presently Ruby Gillis started up to take a sum to the master; she fell back into her seat with a little shriek, believing that her hair was pulled out by the roots. Everybody looked at her and Mr. Phillips glared so sternly that Ruby began to cry. Gilbert had whisked the pin out of sight and was studying his history with the soberest face in the world; but when the commotion subsided he looked at

Anne and winked with inexpressible drollery.

"I think your Gilbert Blythe *is* handsome," confided Anne to Diana, "but I think he's very bold. It isn't good manners to wink at a strange girl."

But it was not until the afternoon that things really began to happen.

Mr. Phillips was back in the corner explaining a problem in algebra to Prissy Andrews and the rest of the scholars were doing pretty much as they pleased eating green apples, whispering, drawing pictures on their slates, and driving crickets harnessed to strings, up and down the aisle. Gilbert Blythe was trying to make Anne Shirley look at him and failing utterly, because Anne was at that moment totally oblivious not only to the very existence of Gilbert Blythe, but of every other scholar in Avonlea school itself. With her chin propped on her hands and her eyes fixed on the blue glimpse of the Lake of Shining Waters that the west window afforded, she was far away in a gorgeous dreamland hearing and seeing nothing save her own wonderful visions.

Gilbert Blythe wasn't used to putting himself out to make a girl look at him and meeting with failure. She *should* look at him, that red-haired Shirley girl with the little pointed chin and the big eyes that weren't like the eyes of any other girl in Avonlea school.

Gilbert reached across the aisle, picked up the end of Anne's long red braid, held it out at arm's length, and said in a piercing whisper: *"Carrots! Carrots!"*

Then Anne looked at him with a vengeance!

She did more than look. She sprang to her feet, her bright fancies fallen into cureless ruin. She flashed one indignant glance at Gilbert from eyes whose angry sparkle was swiftly quenched in equally angry tears.

"You mean, hateful boy!" she exclaimed passionately. "How dare you!"

And then—thwack! Anne had brought her slate down on Gilbert's head and cracked it—slate, not head—clear across.

Avonlea school always enjoyed a scene. This was an especially enjoyable one. Everybody said "Oh" in horrified delight. Diana gasped. Ruby Gillis, who was inclined to be hysterical, began to cry. Tommy Sloane let his team of crickets escape him altogether while he stared open-mouthed at the tableau.

Mr. Phillips stalked down the aisle and laid his hand heavily on Anne's shoulder.

"Anne Shirley, what does this mean?" he said angrily.

Anne returned no answer. It was asking too much of flesh and blood to expect her to tell before the whole school that she had been called "carrots." Gilbert it was who spoke up stoutly.

"It was my fault, Mr. Phillips. I teased her."

Mr. Phillips paid no heed to Gilbert.

"I am sorry to see a pupil of mine displaying such a temper and such a vindictive spirit," he said in a solemn tone, as if the mere fact of being a pupil of his ought to root out all evil passions from the hearts of small imperfect mortals. "Anne, go and stand on the platform in front of the blackboard for the rest of the afternoon."

Anne would have infinitely preferred a whipping to this punishment under which her sensitive spirit quivered as from a whiplash. With a white, set face she obeyed. Mr. Phillips took a chalk crayon and wrote on the blackboard above her head.

"Ann Shirley has a very bad temper. Ann Shirley must learn to control her temper," and then read it out loud so that even the primer class, who couldn't read writing, should understand it.

Anne stood there the rest of the afternoon with that legend above her. She did not cry or hang her head. Anger was still too hot in her heart for that and it sustained her amid all her agony of humiliation. With resentful eyes and passion-red cheeks she confronted alike Diana's sympathetic gaze and Charlie Sloane's indignant nods and

Josie Pye's malicious smiles. As for Gilbert Blythe, she would not even look at him. She would *never* look at him again! She would never speak to him!!

When school was dismissed Anne marched out with her red head held high. Gilbert Blythe tried to intercept her at the porch door.

"I'm awfully sorry I made fun of your hair, Anne," he whispered contritely. "Honest I am. Don't be mad for keeps now."

Anne swept by disdainfully, without look or sign of hearing. "Oh, how could you, Anne?" breathed Diana as they went down the road, half reproachfully, half admiringly. Diana felt that *she* could never have resisted Gilbert's plea.

"I shall never forgive Gilbert Blythe," said Anne firmly. "And Mr. Phillips spelled my name without an *e* too. The iron has entered into my soul, Diana."

Diana hadn't the least idea what Anne meant but she understood it was something terrible.

"You mustn't mind Gilbert making fun of your hair," she said soothingly. "Why, he makes fun of all the girls. He laughs at mine because it's so black. He's called me a crow a dozen times; and I never heard him apologize for anything before, either."

"There's a great deal of difference between being called a crow and being called carrots," said Anne with dignity. "Gilbert Blythe has hurt my feelings *excruciatingly*, Diana."

Thinking About It

1 What will Anne tell Marilla about her day at school? How will *she* tell the story?

2 What does the author, L. M. Montgomery, do to get you on Anne's side in this conflict?

3 As the story continues, say that Anne and Gilbert become friends. How might that happen?

Another Book by L. M. Montgomery

Akin to Anne is a collection of short stories about young people, most of them without families, who triumph over their difficult circumstances.

$3.95 US
$4.95 CDN

Chimney Sweeps

HARPER TROPHY

James Cross Giblin   illustrations by Margot Tomes

from *Chimney Sweeps*
by James Cross Giblin

Climbing Boys

*THERE HAVE BEEN CHIMNEYS ON BUILDINGS
SINCE THE 1100S AND PEOPLE TO CLEAN THEM
FOR AS LONG. BY THE 1500S CHIMNEY SWEEPS,
AS CHIMNEY CLEANERS ARE CALLED, WERE AN
ORGANIZED PROFESSION WITH DISTINCT
CLOTHING AND A LONG TRADITION. BOWING TO
A CHIMNEY SWEEP THREE TIMES AND HAVING A
CHIMNEY SWEEP KISS A NEW BRIDE WERE ONCE
THOUGHT TO BRING GOOD LUCK.*

While superstitions about the luck of
chimney sweeps spread, the real lives of sweeps
in England became harder and harder in the
1700s.

London and other English cities were
growing, and people were building new streets
lined with tall, narrow houses. All the rooms in
these houses needed fireplaces. But the chimney
stack containing the flues from the fireplaces
had to take up as little space as possible.

Architects solved this problem by making the flues smaller. Most of those in the new London houses only measured nine inches by fourteen inches. The flues often ran in a zigzag line through the thick walls of a house to the chimney top. People believed that crooked flues would keep more heat inside the house instead of letting it escape straight up the chimney with the smoke.

At the same time flues were getting smaller and more crooked, more coal was being mined in England. As the supply grew, the price of coal was reduced, and by the late 1700s it replaced wood as the chief heating fuel in England.

All of these changes made it harder to clean chimneys. The soot and creosote from burning logs could easily be swept out of the large older chimneys by servants or chimney sweeps. But the soot from coal fires clung more tightly to the sides of the new, smaller flues and piled up in the corners where the flues made sharp turns.

Adult sweeps were too big to climb up through the narrow flues, and they couldn't get their long-handled brooms around the turns and bends. Only very young boys were small enough to crawl up into the new chimneys and clean out the soot by hand.

These young sweeps were called "climbing boys," and in 1785 it was estimated that there were almost 500 of them in London alone. The boys worked for master sweeps, who were supposed to provide them with food, clothing, and shelter. In 1788, Britain's Parliament passed an act that said climbing boys should be treated as well as any other apprentices. The act also said no children under the age of eight could work as chimney sweeps.

Many master sweeps broke the law, however, and employed children of six, five, and even four years of age. The younger and smaller a child, the more easily he could climb up into the tiny flues, some of which were now only six inches square.

Master sweeps got apprentices from orphanages and sometimes from the children's own parents. In England at the time, there

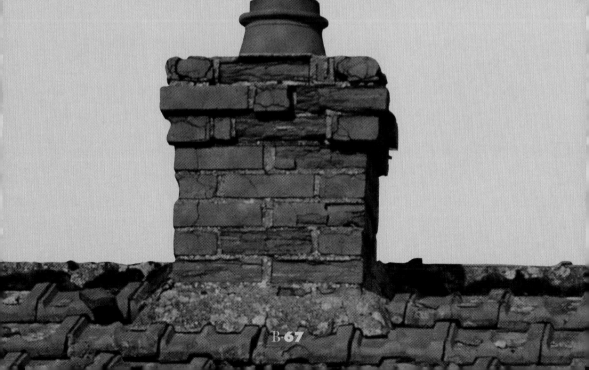

were many poor families with more children than they could afford to feed. Such families were glad to apprentice one of their small sons to a master sweep for five years in return for two or three pounds—about five to eight dollars. The smallest and healthiest boys brought the highest prices.

Some master sweeps did not pay for their apprentices. Instead they kidnapped them from schoolyards and churchyards, or off the streets, and dragged them away to distant parts of the city. It might be years before a kidnapped boy managed to escape and find his way back home again.

If they had children of their own, master sweeps often used them to clean chimneys. Sometimes a master would send one of his little daughters up an especially narrow flue, since girls were usually smaller than boys.

As more masters broke the law and bought or kidnapped little children, English people began to think of chimney sweeps as criminals. They continued to hire master sweeps to clean their chimneys, but they watched with suspicion every move they and their apprentices made while at work in the people's houses.

In Germany at the beginning of the 1800s, few children were employed as sweeps, and most adult chimney sweeps were still treated with respect. In England, however, they were thought to be little better than beggars. They wore hand-me-down clothing and lived in the worst slums. And the sweeps who suffered the most were the youngest—the climbing boys.

A Climbing Boy's Day

What was it like to be a climbing boy in London in 1800?

To understand that, imagine yourself traveling back in time. Then imagine that you are one of three climbing boys working for a master sweep. You are eleven years old and have been cleaning chimneys ever since you were six, when your parents sold you to the master.

It is 4:30 in the morning when the master comes down into the cellar to wake you. You get up every day before dawn because the best time to clean chimneys is in the early morning hours, before people light their fires.

"Get up! Get up!" the master shouts, and the three of you jump up from the burlap bags full of soot that are your only beds. Everyone moves quickly, for you know the master will shake or slap you if you don't.

After stuffing your blanket, which is just a sooty piece of cloth, into an empty burlap bag, you sling the bag over your shoulder. Then you take your cleaning brush and scraper from a shelf above the makeshift beds and follow the master and the other sweeps up the cellar steps.

None of you has to get dressed since you slept in the clothes you wear every day—

a tattered jacket over a gray undershirt, and
black trousers with patches on the knees.
Even though it is October and chilly, the three
of you go barefoot; you have to, for you have
no shoes. In winter, when it's icy, you tie rags
around your feet.

Upstairs, in the single small room where the
master lives, his wife serves breakfast:

two crusts of bread that you dip in a dish of cold gravy left over from the master's supper the night before.

You don't wash your face or hands before eating. There is no running water in the house, and you and the other climbing boys only bathe on Sunday mornings when you carry pails of water from a public well.

After breakfast you grab your bag, brush, and scraper and follow the master and the other sweeps down the stairs to the street. A young journeyman named John joins you there. John was once an apprentice like you, but now at sixteen he is too big to climb chimneys himself. He lives in an attic room in the lodging house and helps the master train new apprentices.

It is still dark outside, but food sellers along the street are already opening their stalls. The smell of freshly baked rolls makes you realize how hungry you are. But the master and John hurry all of you along. Today they want to cover a wealthy neighborhood that's a two-mile walk from where you live.

Peter, the youngest apprentice, soon begins to shiver. By the time you turn down a tree-lined street of brick houses, the little boy's teeth are chattering from the cold. John tells him to keep moving if he wants to stay warm.

"Sweeps! Sweeps here! We'll clean your chimney from the bottom to the top!" the master calls in a loud voice.

A maid runs up from the basement of a house farther down the street and waves to the master. "You've come at just the right time," she says. "We were about to start the kitchen fire."

"My boys and I are always out bright and early," the master says with a wink at John.

"How much do you charge?" the maid asks.

"Twelve pence per flue," the master says.

"Oh, that's too much," the maid replies. "We only paid nine pence a flue the last time we had them cleaned."

"How about ten pence?" the master asks. "My boys do a fine job, and I've got a little fellow to climb the smallest flues." He pats Peter on the shoulder, which only makes the boy shiver more.

"Well, I guess that'll be all right," the maid says. "Our chimney's sorely in need of cleaning. Come in. Come in." She motions for the master and the rest to follow her downstairs into the kitchen of the house.

The master and John drape one of your sooty blanket cloths over the fireplace opening. This will prevent soot and dust from coming out into the kitchen. Then the master tells you to get ready to climb the chimney.

You take off your jacket and shirt and put them on the floor. John gives you a stocking cap with small holes for the eyes to pull down over your face. The knitted cap helps to keep soot from getting into your nose.

Grabbing your brush and scraper, you go behind the blanket drape and look up the chimney. At the top you can see a patch of pale blue sky. Good. The chimney flue is straight and quite wide; it shouldn't be too hard to climb.

First you get a foothold on several of the bricks in the chimney wall. Then, bracing yourself with your elbows and your knees, you inch your way upward. When you first started climbing five years ago, your arms and legs were often rubbed raw by the bricks. Gradually they became covered with thick, hard calluses, and now you don't feel the pain as much.

As you climb, you scrape and brush soot from the chimney's walls and from ledges where it has accumulated. The soot falls all around and down to the hearth below. Despite the stocking cap, some of it gets in your eyes, making you blink, and some of it gets in your nose and mouth too.

At last, twenty minutes after you started climbing, you reach the top of the chimney, fifty feet above the street. "All up!" you shout as you take in great gulps of the cool morning air. Then back down the chimney you climb, scraping and brushing again as you go. You know the master or John will punish you if you dawdle.

Back on the hearth, the other sweeps help you put the fallen soot into one of the burlap sacks. There may be as much as a half bushel. The soot will be carried back to the master's basement and later he'll sell it to farmers for use as fertilizer on their crops.

"Watch that you don't touch anything!" the maid says as she leads you and the other sweeps up the back stairs to the parlor. In it is a fancy fireplace, with a much smaller chimney flue to climb and clean.

The master orders Peter, the youngest apprentice, to climb this one. When the little boy begins to sob, the master turns quickly to Henry, the other sweep, and says, "You'll go up after him to make sure he gets started proper."

Henry nods and leads Peter over to the fireplace, where both boys remove their shirts and put on caps. Peter is still crying, and you know why. You remember what it was like when you were little, and an older sweep, climbing below you, stuck pins in the soles of

your feet to make you keep on going when you were afraid.

Henry and Peter disappear behind the dust cloth that hangs over the mantel, and you can hear them begin to climb. "Get on with it!" Henry shouts.

A few minutes later Henry lifts the cloth and comes into the parlor. "Peter's climbin' nice and smooth," he tells the master. "I only had to poke his feet once."

Peter himself reappears about twenty minutes later. He is black with soot from head to toe, and his elbows and knees show red where they have been scraped by the bricks. But at least he didn't get stuck the way beginners often do. One little boy you worked with got trapped in an especially narrow flue and died from lack of air before he could be rescued.

You and Henry take turns climbing and cleaning the flues in the upstairs bedrooms. They go faster because it's not so far to the roof.

In one room there's a boy about your age, the son of the family that lives in the house. You'd like to talk to him, but he runs away before you have a chance. That's what usually happens with children you meet. Your sooty clothes and face frighten them. Only other climbing boys are able to accept you as you are.

Downstairs again, the maid pays the master for all the flues you and Henry and Peter have climbed. None of you gets any money, but the maid is kinder than some. She gives each of you a hot biscuit just out of the oven and even spreads a bit of butter on top. That's a real treat—it isn't often you taste butter.

"Hurry up, boys!" the master says. He's eager to find more chimneys to clean.

You gulp the rest of your biscuit and sling a bag full of soot over your shoulder. Then you follow the master up the steps and into the street.

"Sweeps! Sweeps here!" John the journey–man calls as you move along.

Before the morning is over, you and the other boys will climb and clean all the flues in two more houses. But that won't be the end of your working day. In the afternoon, after the master has gone home or to his pub, John will lead you and the other sweeps in a search for more chimneys to clean.

The afternoon is the hardest part of the day for you. John makes you work twice as fast because he only gets to keep a small part of what he earns for each flue. The rest he has to give to the master. And often the chimneys you climb are still hot from fires they've had in them earlier in the day.

Once John made you climb a chimney where a fire was blazing in some soot near the top. The higher you went, the hotter it got, and before you finally beat out the flames your face and hands were badly burned.

Luckily, nothing like that happens today and at sundown you trudge home, dragging three bags of soot behind you. Your arms and legs ache, as they do every night, and you're very hungry, and very tired.

Supper, like breakfast, is bread and gravy washed down with a mug of hot tea. "And we have something extra tonight," the master's wife says as she serves up steaming bowls of soup. It's full of leftover vegetables she brought home from the food stall where she works.

"What do you say to that, boys?" the master asks.

"Thank you, ma'am, thank you," you and Henry and Peter reply.

"May I have some more?" Peter asks, and the master's wife refills his bowl halfway. For the first time all day, Peter isn't shivering.

After supper you light a stub of candle and lead the way down into the cellar. It is only 7:30, but everyone is too tired to play or even to talk.

You lie down on the bags of soot you collected during the day and snuff out the candle. Before long you can hear Henry and little Peter breathing heavily in sleep.

You know you should get to sleep yourself. Soon it will be 4:30 in the morning again, and the master will be calling for you to "Get up and be quick about it!"

But tonight memories of your family fill your mind. Often there wasn't enough to eat, or any wood for the fireplace, but at least you were all together—your father and mother, your brothers and sisters, and you. "Will we ever be together again?" you wonder silently. "Or will I just go on climbing chimneys forever?"

Turning over on the lumpy sack, you make yourself as comfortable as possible and finally fall asleep.

Help for Climbing Boys

While English climbing boys lived through days like the one just described, and thought no one cared about them, some people in London were trying to find ways to help them.

In 1803, a wealthy gentleman became concerned about young sweeps after a climbing boy was caught in his chimney and had to be dug out. With a group of friends, the man formed a society to improve the working conditions of apprentice chimney sweeps. The society hired inspectors to investigate all the master sweeps in the city. The inspectors were supposed to make sure that the law was being obeyed and that no children under the age of eight were employed as climbing boys.

To get a more complete picture of the lives of climbing boys, the society held a series of hearings. They invited master sweeps, climbing boys, and doctors who had treated them to come to the hearings and tell about their experiences.

From their testimony, the society members discovered that most climbing boys suffered from one or more serious ailments. Some boys had badly swollen eyelids or weak sight because they were constantly rubbing soot out of their eyes. Many caught colds, asthma, or tuberculosis from being out in the cold and exposed day after day to dust and soot. Others had crooked spines or deformed arms and legs because they had been made to climb chimneys when their bones were still soft and growing.

Worst of all, many boys were victims of the terrible disease known as "chimney sweeps' cancer." Since weeks often went by between washings, soot would accumulate in the boys' crotches and irritate the skin. Instead of healing, these sores sometimes hardened into cancerous lumps. If the lumps weren't discovered and removed in time, the boys might die.

The society members learned that only one climbing boy in ten knew how to read or write. A few were taken to Sunday school by their masters, but none could go to regular school because they were busy cleaning chimneys in the morning. Besides, few schools wanted the dirty, shabby climbing boys as pupils.

When the boys reached the age of twelve or thirteen and got too big to climb chimneys, most of them were not fit for any other work. Some older boys helped their former masters train apprentices and later became master sweeps themselves. A few went to sea as sailors. Some were so sick and deformed they could only wander the streets as beggars. Others turned to crime.

After hearing all the testimony, the society decided that no children of any age should be forced to work as chimney sweeps. But what could replace them? The answer had to be some kind of machine.

The society offered a prize of 40 guineas (about $200 today) to the person who could invent a successful chimney-sweeping machine. The winning design was submitted by a man named George Smart and featured a round brush large enough to rub against all four sides of a nine-by-fourteen-inch flue. The brush was attached to the top of a short, hollow stick.

As the brush was thrust up the chimney, more sticks were added to the first, each fitting neatly into the one above it. Finally the brush reached the chimney top. Then it was worked down again slowly so that the flue got a double cleaning.

The society had the device tested and an architect reported that three-quarters of the chimneys in London could be cleaned with it. The rest of the chimneys could easily be altered

A nineteenth-century engraving of George Smart's chimney-cleaning machine

Modern chimney-cleaning tools

so that the special brushes could be used in them too.

The results encouraged the society to take its case to the highest levels of English government.

In 1804, its supporters offered Parliament a bill urging that the use of climbing boys be outlawed. The bill listed all the evidence the society had gathered about the cruel conditions in which the boys lived and worked. Then it described the new cleaning device and explained how it could replace the boys.

The bill met with strong opposition. Master sweeps feared that they would no longer be able to earn a living if others learned to operate the cleaning device. And homeowners feared that the device would be more expensive than climbing boys, especially if their chimneys had to be rebuilt to accommodate it.

Parliament listened to these arguments, and the bill was defeated. But the society did not give up. It gathered more evidence and introduced new bills in Parliament in 1817 and again in 1819.

At the same time, people began protesting other kinds of child labor in England. New factories, mines, and mills were springing up all over the country, and children were being hired to work in them at low wages. In 1816, the reformer and educator Robert Owen proposed that only children above the age of twelve be employed in textile mills and that they work no more than ten hours a day. His suggestions were ignored by the mill owners, but more and more people came to believe that child labor was wrong.

In 1833, Parliament finally passed a bill prohibiting the employment of children under the age of nine in mills and factories. That bill limited the working hours of children ages nine to twelve to eight per day and those of young people ages thirteen to eighteen to sixty-nine per week. The same law raised the minimum age for apprentice climbing boys from eight to ten. And it required that all chimneys in England be altered so that they could be cleaned with extension poles and brushes.

These were important steps forward, but the society still was not satisfied. It continued to press in Parliament for more laws to protect climbing boys. Famous authors like Charles Dickens joined in the fight by writing about the hard life of chimney sweeps in *Oliver Twist* and other books. At last, in 1840, a bill was passed forbidding young men under the age of twenty-one to climb and clean flues as a profession.

The society's struggle wasn't over yet, however. Despite the new laws, master sweeps kept on using children as climbing boys, and there weren't enough policemen or inspectors to stop them. It wasn't until 1875 that Parliament established strict regulations for the licensing of chimney sweeps. When they applied for a license, all master sweeps had to list the names and ages of their apprentices. No longer could they employ small children in secret.

At last the society could relax. For this law finally ended the use of climbing boys in England—a practice that had injured or killed hundreds of children each year for more than a century.

Writing: An Adventure of Discovery

BY JAMES CROSS GIBLIN

When I was in school, I liked to act in plays and wanted to learn how to write them. Later, in college, I studied play-writing and did write some plays. But then I became an editor of children's books and spent most of my time helping other writers to write better. I hadn't forgotten my dramatic training, though. When I began to write nonfic-tion books like *Chimney Sweeps*, I used it to help bring my material to life.

For example, part of this selection, "A Climbing Boy's Day," is based on statements of real chimney sweeps in nineteenth century London. After reading their statements, I decided to create a group of fictional climbing boys and follow them through a typical work day. I made up dialogue for them to say, just as I used to make up dialogue for the characters in my plays. However, all the details—the clothes the boys wore, the way they cleaned chimneys, the soot-filled sacks on which they slept—are true.

Writing books like *Chimney Sweeps* is an adventure of discovery for me, and it begins with getting the idea. The idea for *Chimney Sweeps* came to me in a most unusual way. I was  flying to Oklahoma City on business and sat next to a young man who happened to be a chimney sweep and a manufacturer of the folding brooms that sweeps use today. As he told me about his profession and its history, I thought, "This might make an interesting book."

Doing research for a book is a lot like playing detective. I start by compiling a list of topics I want to explore in the book and the places where I think I might find information on each of them. Libraries provide me with much of this information. When I was researching *Chimney Sweeps,* I spent long hours in the New York Public Library and the Library of Congress in Washington, D.C. It was exciting to turn a page in a book or magazine and find just the fact I'd been looking for.

Many people think that nonfiction books are dull and boring. Obviously I don't agree with them. I believe it can be just as thrilling to read about the fight for pure milk or the hard lives of child chimney sweeps as it is to read a mystery story. That's why I've written nonfiction books about these and other subjects, and why I look forward to writing many more.

Thinking About It

1. Suddenly, the year is 1750 and you are a climbing boy. You can have two minutes to talk across the centuries to tell about yourself. What is most important to tell?

2. In 1803, a wealthy gentleman and his friends formed a society to improve the conditions of climbing boys. Why would they want to help the boys?

3. A climbing boy from England in 1795 gets into a time machine and comes to visit you. He is with you for one whole day, a day that, for you, is a typical school day. What surprises the climbing boy?

Another Book by James Cross Giblin
Why do you eat with a fork? *From Hand to Mouth: Or, How We Invented Knives, Forks, Spoons, and Chopsticks and the Table Manners to Go with Them* is a fascinating look at eating utensils.

from Morning Star, Black Sun
by Brent Ashabranner

THEY WILL TEAR UP THE EARTH

The Tribal Council chambers at Lame Deer were overcrowded and hot on that July day in 1972. Cheyenne from all over the reservation sat silently in their chairs and waited to hear the representatives of Consolidation Coal Company, known as Consol, explain the company's new offer. Most people in the room already had heard rumors of it, but the figures were so big that they were hard to understand.

The Consol team was large, and finally the leader stood up. He smiled and began to talk, first reminding the listeners that his company already had bid on and received a coal exploration permit and leasing rights on fifteen thousand acres of Cheyenne land. The agreement was the same as for all other companies:

17 1/2 cents a ton for coal shipped off the reserva–
tion, 15 cents for coal used on the reservation.

Now, he said, Consol was ready immediately
to make the Cheyenne tribe a new offer. The
company would increase the royalty on all coal
mined to 25 cents a ton, regardless of whether
it was used on or off the reservation. The
company would pay a bonus of $35 an acre for
all land mined. Finally, Consol would make a
donation of $1.5 million toward the building
of a health center that the Northern Cheyenne
so badly needed.

But there would be conditions to this offer.
For such a high royalty and large bonus, the
tribe would have to agree to let Consolidation
Coal Company lease seventy thousand acres
of reservation land and mine at least one
billion tons of coal. The company
would also have to be allowed to build
four plants on the reservation. These
plants would turn coal into gas, just as
generating plants turn coal into electricity.
The process of gasification takes a great
deal of water, so the tribe would have to
agree to let reservation water be used in
the plants.

The Consol representative reminded his
listeners that the Cheyenne would make a
great deal of money from the company's offer.
The total royalty on a billion tons of coal would
be $250 million. The gasification plants would

bring much more money onto the
reservation and would mean lots of jobs.
The Cheyenne would certainly become
one of the richest Indian tribes
in America.

Ted Risingsun was in the audience
that day when the amazing Consol
offer was explained. He remembers breaking
into a sweat at the thought of all that money
and what he could do with his share of it.
But Ted had heard some things about plant
building and gasification that he thought his
fellow Cheyenne ought to know, so when a
chance came, he stood up to talk.

"Well," he said, "that sure is a lot of money.
I've heard that every member of the tribe might
get $150,000. And I've heard a few whispers
that maybe someday every Cheyenne might
even be a millionaire.

"I've been sitting here thinking about what
I'd do with all that money, and it's so much I
don't really know. But I think one thing I
might do is buy myself the most expensive
elkskin scalp shirt anybody ever had. You know
how our ancestors used to tie scalps on their
scalp shirts. Well, I would tie pieces of coal on
mine. I'd buy myself the biggest pink Cadillac I
could find. Then I'd drive around the country
and dance in all the Indian powwows."

The Cheyenne in the room listened quietly.
Knowing Ted Risingsun, they knew he had

something else on his mind. "But then," Ted continued, "I got to thinking about where I would go when I finished all that dancing. I doubt if I could come back here. We've already leased or given permits to lease over half of our land. If we lease seventy thousand more acres to Consol, there won't be much left. But maybe that's not the main thing. I've heard that to build those gasification plants and run them and take out the coal for them there will be ten white people working and living on this reservation for every Cheyenne here. If that happens, I don't think there will be a Cheyenne tribe any more.

"Now most of us are poor. I don't have to tell anyone in this room about that. But we have these hills and grass and trees and streams, and if we don't give them away, no one can take them away from us. We've got our tribe's whole history and culture right here. So maybe we're not so poor. But even if we are, I think I would rather be poor in my own country, with my own people, with our own way of life than be rich in a torn-up land where I am outnumbered ten to one by strangers."

It was probably the longest speech Ted Risingsun had ever made, and he could tell from the looks on the faces of his neighbors and friends and some who maybe were not friends that they had heard every word. He knew that the team from Consol had heard, too, because one of them said that the company had to have an answer by the next day or the offer would be withdrawn. Then they left.

The Cheyenne Tribal Council did not answer Consol the next day or any time soon, but the company did not withdraw the offer. It was an offer that sent shock waves through the Tribal Council and into every Cheyenne home. For the first time the Indians of this small and isolated tribe began to understand what leasing their land to a big coal company would lead to. It was not only the stripping bare of a large part of their land to rip out the coal, though that was bad enough. But the companies didn't want the coal unless they could build generating or gasification plants at the "mine mouth," as company officials expressed it. Then would come the miners, plant builders, plant operators, and their families, and the Cheyenne would become a minority group on their own reservation.

The Consol offer had done another thing. It had shown the Cheyenne how poorly they had fared financially under the guidance of the Bureau of Indian Affairs. Consol did not go through the Bureau with its new offer but rather took it directly to the Cheyenne Tribal Council. On the BIA's advice the Council had accepted a 12-cent-an-acre bonus from the

Peabody Coal Company, and now Consol was offering them $35 an acre! More important, Consol offered 25 cents a ton royalty on the coal instead of 17 ½ cents or 15 cents that all previous leases had called for.

And now it was clear why the coal companies had insisted on that lower royalty of 15 cents for coal burned on the reservation. Their secret plans called for them to burn as much Cheyenne coal as possible on the reservation. The Tribal Council learned that Peabody had plans to mine five hundred million or more tons of coal from their Cheyenne leases and supply it to gasification plants that would be built on or near the reservation by the Northern Gas Company and the City Service Gas Company.

The Tribal Council could understand that in 1966 the BIA might not have known or even guessed at what the coal and power companies' long-range plans were. What the Indians could not understand was why, in time and as interest in Indian coal increased, the Bureau did not learn what was afoot. The BIA, after all, is a part of the Department of the Interior, and it was the Department of the Interior that took the leading role in the *North Central Power Study.* How could two parts of the same department, both concerned with coal in Montana, have no knowledge of what the other was doing?

In a statement before a congressional committee several years later, Allen Rowland, the Council's president, summed up the Cheyenne feeling about the Bureau in these words: "It soon became apparent that the involved BIA personnel, on whose advice and counsel the tribe relied in entering into these transactions, had been inept, uninformed, and sadly overmatched."

Now it was clear to the Cheyenne leaders that the wheel of history had come full circle. There was a terrible symmetry between what had happened to their forefathers a hundred years ago and what was happening to them now. Then the white man had wanted their land for farms and ranches and for the gold beneath the Dakota Black Hills. The government had sent the army cavalry to drive them off the land.

This time, a century later, it was coal that the white man wanted. This time it was not ranchers and farmers and prospectors who came but well-dressed businessmen and lawyers. This time the government could not send the army, for the Cheyenne had legal title to this small piece of land. But the government, in the form of the Bureau of Indian Affairs, could help the businessmen, and it did.

Once again the elders of the Cheyenne tribe recalled the prophecy of Sweet Medicine: "The white people will try to change you from

your way of living to theirs, and they will keep at what they try to do. They will tear up the earth and at last you will do it with them. When you do this, you will become crazy and will forget all that I have taught you. Then you will disappear."

The prophecy hung with heavy menace over the heads of the tribal leaders, for now they could see the scarred and torn-up earth around Colstrip only a few miles away. And they themselves had agreed to let the white man tear up Cheyenne land in the same way. *They will tear up the earth and at last you will do it with them."*

Then the tribal leaders knew that they must act. Perhaps these descendants of Little Wolf and Dull Knife did not hear ancestral voices crying war. Perhaps they did not smoke the medicine pipe and seek guidance in the dreams it brought as Two Moons might have done before the Battle of the Little Bighorn. But they knew one thing: it was time once more for the Cheyenne to fight.

THINKING ABOUT IT

1. You are a Northern Cheyenne at the Tribal Council meeting. You don't have much money, but you have a proud past and you hear that perhaps you could be wealthy in the future. What are your thoughts as you listen to Ted Risingsun speak?

2. You have read nonfiction articles by James Cross Giblin and Brent Ashabranner. What do you think these authors had to do before they wrote these articles? What did they have to do while they were writing?

3. "We want to change your community. We want to improve your way of living," say some people called developers. What will you need to find out before you agree or disagree to let them do what they have in mind?

Another Book About Native Americans

Sitting Bull and the Plains Indians, by Jason Hook, is an informative look at the history, customs, and life of several groups of Native Americans, including the Cheyenne.

THE REAL WOLF

by Jane Rockwell

From the beginning we hear many dreadful things about wolves.

Remember the wolf that made life miserable for The Three Little Pigs? Do you recall the story of Peter and the Wolf in which a clever boy outsmarted a blood-thirsty wolf? And who can forget the wolf that almost tricked Little Red Riding Hood into becoming his dinner?

> As far back as the sixth century B.C., ... the wolf was portrayed as an evil animal.

As far back as the sixth century B.C., when we think Aesop's fables were written, the wolf was portrayed as an evil animal. At least twenty-two tales in the fables describe the deceit, wicked-ness, and thievery of the wolf. Later, in Roman times, the satirist Petronius wrote about the horrors of the werewolf. The word *berserk* comes from the Norse word, *berserker,* which meant someone who wore the skin of a wolf and performed terrible "beast-like" acts, as a werewolf. In the Middle Ages, when witchcraft was popular, people accused of lycanthropy —assuming the form and traits of wolves—were condemned and burned to death.

Only two classic tales in literature speak well of the wolf. One is the legend of Romulus and Remus, the founders of Rome, who, in their infancy, were cared for by a mother wolf. The other appears in Rudyard Kipling's *The Jungle Book*. It is the story of Mowgli, a boy who was raised by a she-wolf named Raksha.

There is evidence also that the American Indians, in some cases, thought highly of the wolf. Warriors were named after them, and a mountain in Glacier National Park in Montana was named Rising Wolf Mountain in memory of a trapper whom the Blackfoot Indians considered to be as wise as a wolf.

Other than fairy tales, we read, see, and hear more stories about wolves with fierce jaws and long, sharp teeth that prey upon innocent people and helpless animals. Cartoons and comic strips portray the wolf as an animal to be feared. Movies and TV dramatize the deeds of werewolves—creatures which, at certain times, change to wolves and terrify all those in sight—and the awesome Wolfman.

Our language includes many sayings that cast the wolf in the role of villain. **"A wolf in sheep's clothing,"** for example, is someone who conceals his or her evil character by pretending innocence. **"Cry wolf"** means to give a false alarm. **"Wolfing down a meal"** suggests a person who is greedy and ill-mannered. The phrase **"throw it to the wolves"** comes from the

> Our language includes many sayings that cast the wolf in the role of villain.

days when the horse and cart was the main source of transportation. To protect himself and his horse from hungry wolves, the driver, as legend has it, would throw food to the wolves and then hurry on to his destination. The wolves would stop to eat the food, and the horse and driver would be spared. And a human **"wolf"** is a male who **"preys"** upon innocent

females. His **"howls"** are called wolf whistles, or wolf calls.

Even some dictionaries define the wolf's habits as **"cruel, fierce, and greedy."**

Everyone, it would seem, is threatened in some way by this awful beast.

Fiction, not Fact

Because stories, movies, and other forms of fiction are the only means most people have to learn about wolves, they have no choice but to believe that all of these dreadful things about wolves are true. It is hard to realize that these notions about wolves are fiction, not fact.

The friendship between humans and wolves began to fade as people's needs changed.

Why does the wolf have such a bad reputation? By the time you have read this article, I hope you will know why the wolf is so misunderstood. More important, I hope you will discover that the "real wolf" is a fine, noble animal that deserves to keep its rightful place in the animal kingdom.

Wolves and Human History

Thousands of years ago wolves roamed freely over the earth. Unlike today, they could live and hunt wherever they pleased. Their main source of food was animals moving in herds. These animals were the ancestors of buffaloes, antelopes, moose, and deer.

Centuries ago, people, like wolves, depended on herd animals for food. To round up and catch their common prey, wolves and humans formed a kind of partnership. When they weren't hunting on their own in the wild, wolves helped primitive people track down or ambush these fleet-footed animals. For their efforts they were allowed to feed on leftover bones and meat scraps discarded by humans. The wolves' young—called pups—probably played with

the children of primitive man and woman.

The friendship between humans and wolves began to fade as people's needs changed. As early man and woman became civilized and moved about the world, their lives became more complicated. No longer did they depend so much on wild animals for game. They planted crops and raised many different kinds of animals for food. They also trained some of these animals to till their land and help them with other outside chores. Less independent than the wolf, dogs were domesticated and trained to herd sheep, goats, and other animals and to guard human property and possessions.

To stay alive, wolves turned to smaller animals, including those raised by humans, such as sheep, goats, and chickens.

War on Wolves

As men, women, and their children populated more areas of the earth, their needs and demands became even greater. Guns and other weapons were invented to hunt wild animals for sport as well as for food and protection. In time, the wolves' prey—vast herds of buffaloes, caribou, moose, and other large, grazing animals—began to disappear. To stay alive, wolves turned to smaller animals, including those raised by humans, such as sheep, goats, and chickens. Wolves became rivals and, soon, enemies of people. To protect their property, humans hunted and killed wolves in ever-increasing numbers or offered bounties — payments of money or goods—to trappers and hunters to do it for them.

Farms, ranches, and later, cities, replaced the wolves' hunting territories. They were driven into wilderness areas where it was possible to hide from humans and their deadly weapons.

Wolves still live mainly in the wilderness, but their numbers have decreased drastically throughout the world. Aside from some national forests and refuge lands where they are protected by law, there are very few wolves left compared to the time they ranged over most of the earth.

By 1509 the wolf was no longer in England. In 1743 it had disappeared from Scotland, and by 1776 it was no longer seen in Ireland. From 1915 to 1935 wolves were exterminated from most of the United States by the Federal government. Since the 1960s in eastern Europe and the Soviet Union, thousands of wolves are killed every year in large wolf extermination programs.

Because the wolf was—and still is—considered a threat to human beings and their property, tales, mostly false, spread throughout the world and were accepted as true by most people. The idea of the big, bad wolf—created by humans—had come to stay.

From 1915 to 1935 wolves were exterminated from most of the United States by the Federal government.

THINKING ABOUT IT

1. What did this article do to your opinion of wolves?

2. *Wolves have been treated unfairly.* What evidence does this article give to support that statement?

3. This book, *Look Both Ways,* is about resolving differences. What could be done to ease the tensions between wolves and people?

The
Grandmother
by Sara Henderson Hay

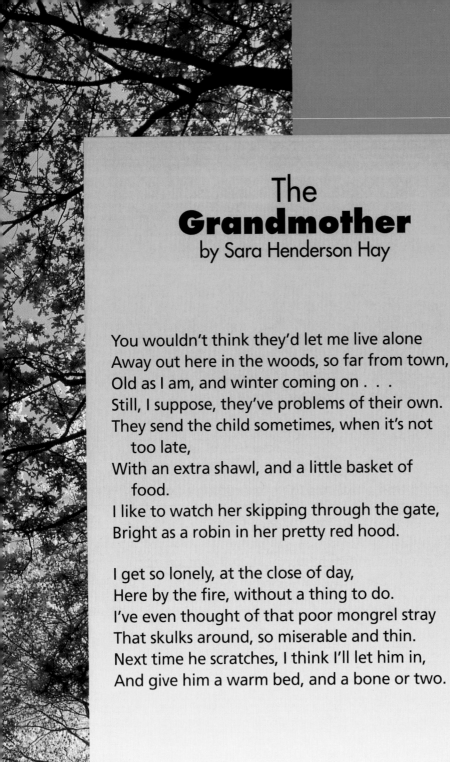

You wouldn't think they'd let me live alone
Away out here in the woods, so far from town,
Old as I am, and winter coming on . . .
Still, I suppose, they've problems of their own.
They send the child sometimes, when it's not
    too late,
With an extra shawl, and a little basket of
    food.
I like to watch her skipping through the gate,
Bright as a robin in her pretty red hood.

I get so lonely, at the close of day,
Here by the fire, without a thing to do.
I've even thought of that poor mongrel stray
That skulks around, so miserable and thin.
Next time he scratches, I think I'll let him in,
And give him a warm bed, and a bone or two.

The
Builders
by Sara Henderson Hay

I told them a thousand times if I told them
    once:
Stop fooling around, I said, with straw and
    sticks;
They won't hold up. You're taking an awful chance.
Brick is the stuff to build with, solid bricks.
You want to be impractical, go ahead.
But just remember, I told them; wait and see,
You're making a big mistake. Awright, I said,
But when the wolf comes, don't come running to me.

The funny thing is, they didn't. There they sat,
One in his crummy yellow shack, and one
Under his roof of twigs, and the wolf ate
Them, hair and hide. Well, what is done is done.
But I'd been willing to help them, all along,
If only they'd once admitted they were wrong.

The Trial of
THE BIG BAD WOLF

by Val R. Cheatham

from *Plays Magazine*

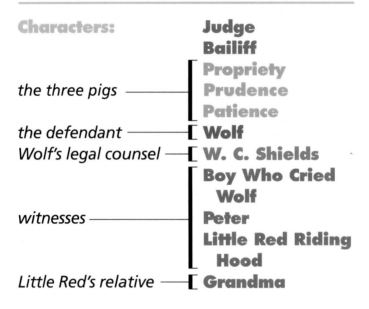

Characters:

	Judge
	Bailiff
the three pigs	Propriety / Prudence / Patience
the defendant	Wolf
Wolf's legal counsel	W. C. Shields
witnesses	Boy Who Cried Wolf / Peter / Little Red Riding Hood
Little Red's relative	Grandma

Setting: *Courtroom. Judge's bench is left. Pitcher of water, glass, 3 or 4 ice bags, and gavel are on bench. Table is next to bench. Facing bench are two small tables with chairs. A row of chairs for witnesses is up right.*

At rise: Three Pigs *sit at one table,* Wolf *and* W. C. Shields, *who is sleeping, sit at the other.* Peter, Little Red Riding Hood, *and* Boy Who Cried Wolf *sit in chairs up right.* Bailiff, *carrying papers, enters, goes to table, picks up gavel.*

Bailiff *(Pounding gavel):* Hear ye! Hear ye! All rise, please. *(All rise.* Judge *enters, carrying ice bag.)* The highly esteemed, 37th court of the prestigious district, presided over by the most honorable, his eminence, the Judge.

Judge *(Interrupting; annoyed):* All right, already! That's enough! I have a splitting headache! Just get on with it. *(Sits at bench)*

Bailiff *(Loudly):* Be seated! *(All sit.)*

Judge *(Aside):* It's going to be another long day. *(To* Bailiff*)* What's on the docket? *(Pounds gavel, then holds head)* Ohh! My head!

Bailiff *(Reading from paper):* Today on the docket we have the three pigs, Pretentious, Pompous, and Presumptuous.

Propriety *(Interrupting):* That's Propriety . . .

Prudence: Prudence . . .

Patience: And Patience.

Bailiff: Oh? Whatever. The Three Pigs, here, have brought suit against the Wolf.

Propriety: That's Big,

Prudence: Bad,

Patience: Wolf.

Wolf *(Rising):* I object! I object!
(Nudges W. C., *who wakes up, rubs eyes)*
Tell them I'm not a big bad wolf.

W.C. *(Rising and speaking in manner of W. C. Fields):* Ah, yes, Your Honor, as anyone can see, my client is neither big nor bad. In fact, my client the Wolf won the American Dental Society's Seal of Customer Promotion for giving candy to children.

Judge *(Annoyed):* Sit down until the trial starts. *(Pounds gavel, then groans, and slaps ice bag on head)* Continue, Bailiff. (W. C. *sits, goes back to sleep.*)

Bailiff *(Reading from paper):* The Three Pigs have charged the Wolf with assault and battery, trespassing, and destruction of property.

Wolf: I object! I object!

Bailiff *(Rapping gavel):* Sit down, Wolf! You can't object.

Judge: I object to both of you. Sit down and stop being so loud. *(Rubs head)* Why didn't my law professors tell me there would be days like this? *(To* Three Pigs*)* Get on with it.

Propriety: Of course.

Prudence: As you wish.

Patience: Yes, Your Honor.

Propriety *(Rising):* You see, we three simple, unassuming pigs were having a nice, quiet evening at home.

Prudence: All of a sudden we heard a thunderous knock at our door.

Patience *(Excitedly):* We peeked out the window, and what did we see?

Boy Who Cried Wolf *(Jumping up):* The Wolf! The Wolf! I know it was the Wolf!

Pigs *(Together):* Right. The big, bad Wolf! *(They point at* Wolf.*)*

Wolf: I object! I object! *(Gesturing at* Boy*)* This boy has cried "Wolf!" many times before. *(To* W. C.*)* Wake up! *(Nudges* W. C.*)* Tell them we object!

W.C. *(Waking up):* Huh? Oh, yes. *(To* Judge*)* Of course, we object, Your Honor. Anyone can see my client is neither big nor bad. In fact, my client the Wolf won the American Dental Society's Seal of Customer Promotion for giving candy—

Wolf *(Interrupting):* You already told them that.

W.C. *(Confused):* I did? Ah, yes . . . so I did. Have I said, Your Honor, that my client has never once tripped an old lady while a Boy Scout was helping her across the street?

Little Red Riding Hood: What about my grandma? I took a basket of goodies through the woods to her house and all I found was the Wolf!

Boy: The Wolf is guilty! The Wolf is guilty!

Peter: Yes! He chased me through the deep snow all over Russia. And, that's a lot of chasing!

Boy: The Wolf is guilty!

Bailiff *(Banging gavel):* Quiet! Quiet!

Judge *(Getting another ice bag):* Bailiff, must you always shout? *(Indicates witnesses)* Who are these people?

Bailiff: They are witnesses, Your Honor— witnesses for the prosecution.

Judge: They shouldn't be shouting.

Red Riding Hood *(Rising)*: Your Honor, I'm Little Red Riding Hood. I went through the woods to Grandma's house, and found the Wolf propped up on the couch, eating a TV dinner and watching Saturday morning cartoons. We don't know what happened to Grandma!

Peter *(Rising):* I'm Peter, from "Peter and the Wolf." The Wolf ate a duck that was swimming in a pond near my house. It was a cold, premeditated act.

Wolf *(Hands on hips; angrily):* You've got a lot of nerve complaining about me, Peter, when you're the one who gets top billing.

Boy *(Rising):* I'm the boy who cried "Wolf!" I called the townspeople to come and save the sheep from the Wolf.

Judge: Sit down, all of you! *(Pounds gavel)* Sit! Sit! Sit! Silence! *(Groans)* Oh, my aching head.

Bailiff *(Loudly):* All sit in the courtroom! Silence!

Judge *(To* Bailiff*):* You be silent, too *(Calmly)* Now, we are here to try the Wolf, not my patience, as some of you seem to be doing. And we are trying him only for crimes against the Three Little Pigs. I want to hear only

words relevant to that case, and *(Lowers voice)* no words spoken louder than this. Do you understand? *(Looks at* Pigs, *who nod, then at* W. C., *who is sleeping.* Wolf *nudges* W. C.*)*

W.C. *(Waking up):* Huh?

Wolf: The Judge wants us to be quiet.

W.C. *(Rising):* Quiet? Why, Your Honor, there is no one in the world who can be quieter than my client, the stealthy Wolf. *(*Wolf *gestures for* W. C. *to be quiet.)* Why, he can sneak up on an unsuspecting person without making a sound.

Wolf *(Pulling* W. C. *back to his seat):* Not now! Be quiet!

Boy *(Rising):* Yes, sneak—that's what the Wolf does, he sneaks!

Judge *(Cautioning):* Ah-ah-ah! *(Gestures to him to be silent.* Boy *sits.)* Now, Pigs, continue your testimony.

Propriety: Yes, Your Honor. The Wolf banged on our door and demanded to be let in.

Prudence: We told him, "Not by the hair of your chinny-chin-chin."

Patience: That's when he proceeded to huff and puff and blow our house down.

Wolf (Leaping to feet): Wrong

W.C. (Awakening and jumping up): I object, Your Honor. Anyone can plainly see my client is not a windbag.

Wolf (Interrupting): Never mind. I'll tell what really happened. (W. C. dozes again.) I was out jogging—you know, healthy body, sound mind—when I passed the Three Pigs' house. I thought it would be nice to pay a little social call on them, so I started walking up to their front door. Little did I know that they have goldenrod all around their house! I'm allergic to goldenrod, and I started sneezing. I just couldn't stop! I sneezed so hard, in fact, that the Pigs' flimsy little house toppled over! It was an accident!

Peter (Rising): Well, it was no accident when you chased me all over Russia in the deep snow.

Wolf: I chased you? Now, really, Peter. I was only trying to stop you and tell you to button your coat. I knew your mother would be worried about you with all that blowing snow.

Red Riding Hood: Worried? I'm the one who's worried. My grandma is still missing. I haven't seen her since the Wolf paid one of his little social visits on her.

Wolf: Young lady, I can assure you that your grandmother is fine.

Boy: The Wolf did it! The Wolf did it! She's lost and it's all the Wolf's fault!

Witnesses *(Ad lib):* Right! The Wolf is guilty! No doubt about it. *(Etc.)*

Judge *(Pounding gavel):* Silence!

Bailiff *(Holding hands over ears):* Ohh! That really does cause a headache, doesn't it? *(To Judge)* May I borrow your ice bag? *(Reaches for Judge's ice bag. Judge taps Bailiff's hand with gavel.)*

Judge: Get your own! *(Wearily)* Now, we're going to finish this trial very quickly, one way or the other. Is there anyone left who hasn't testified?

W.C. *(Awakening):* I object, Your Honor!

Judge: Not you, counselor! Sit down!

Grandma *(Tottering in):* You haven't heard from me yet.

Red Riding Hood *(Rushing over to Grandma):* Grandma! Where have you been? Are you all right?

Grandma *(Crossing to center):* Of course, I'm all right. In fact, I'm better than all right—have been for 90 years. *(To Wolf)* There you are! You promised to take me disco dancing. *(Does dance steps)* Hurry up and get this over with so we can move it and groove it!

Wolf *(Stammering):* Wait a minute. I, ah—that is—I can't. You see, I hurt my right leg jogging over to the Pigs' house the other night. My left foot is, ah—is frostbitten, because I was chasing—that is, trying to help poor little Peter, who was out in the deep snow with his coat unbuttoned.

Judge *(Rapping gavel):* That's enough! I've heard all I need to know. Wolf, approach the bench. *(Wolf crosses to bench. Judge hands him envelope.)* I want you to appear at this address next Friday evening. *(Raps gavel)* Case dismissed!

Wolf *(Studying envelope):* But, Judge, if the case is dismissed, why must I appear next Friday night?

Judge: The envelope contains the address and entrance rules for the Liar's Club. I think you'll win first prize for me next Friday.

Grandma: Come on, Wolfie, let's go boogie! *(Dances)*

Wolf *(Holding up hands with wrists together, as if for handcuffs):* Arrest me! I'd rather be in jail! *(Quick curtain)*

THE END

"Arrest me!"

Pulling the Theme Together

Resolving Conflict

1. You are the judge in the court. Is the Wolf guilty or innocent of the charge? You are also a member of the Liar's Club. Does the Wolf win first prize? Explain your rulings.

2. What would a peer mediator do about the dispute between the Wolf and the Three Pigs?

3. The people, animals, and groups in *Look Both Ways* get together to discuss what, if anything, they've learned about resolving differences. What do they tell each other? What can you tell them?

Books to Enjoy

Chevrolet Saturdays
by Candy Dawson Boyd
Macmillan, 1993
It's a tough year for Joey Davis. He has to deal with a teacher who doesn't like him, a class bully, and–hardest of all–a new stepfather. He can handle school. It's proving himself to his stepfather that will be a challenge.

No Beasts! No Children!
Beverly Keller
Harper, 1983
Desdemona's landlord says he doesn't rent to people with pets. Desdemona's family has three dogs, a mouse, a cat, and a strange beast in the backyard. Is there a problem here?

The Bully of Barkham Street
by Mary Stolz
Harper, 1963
Martin has earned a reputation as a bully. At first, he doesn't seem to care, but now he wants to change what people think of him. He soon finds out how hard that is to do.

Milk: The Fight for Purity
by James Cross Giblin
Crowell, 1986
Drinking milk was once hazardous to your health. This history of the battle to produce cleaner milk is exciting and ongoing.

Anthony Burns: The Defeat and Triumph of a Fugitive Slave
by Virginia Hamilton
Knopf, 1988
This biography is both the story of a former slave's fight for his own freedom and the story of the anti-slavery movement's fight for freedom for all.

Gray Wolf, Red Wolf
by Dorothy Hinshaw Patent
Clarion, 1990
The gray wolf and the red wolf, both native to North America, are fighting for their survival. Is there anything you can do to help?

Murphy's Island
by Colleen McKenna
Scholastic, 1990
When the Murphys move to Put-in-Bay Island for the school year, eleven-year-old Colleen's biggest challenge will be to overcome the islanders' unfriendly attitude.

Literary Terms

Expository Nonfiction

Expository nonfiction is writing that explains something. "Climbing Boys" explains clearly how child chimney sweeps were treated and the work they had to do. Much of the information is given through descriptions of their work day. "They Will Tear Up the Earth" describes the choice the Cheyenne faced about the use of their land.

Idiom

An idiom is a phrase that means something different from the literal meaning of the words. In "Peer Mediation" Rachel tells Josh and Herb that one of the rules is that they can't "put each other down." Rachel doesn't mean that they might physically put each other down on the ground as if they were fighting. She's telling them that they aren't allowed to verbally insult each other during the mediation session.

Imagery

Imagery is the use of words that help a reader experience the way things look, sound, smell, taste, or feel. In "A Tempest in the School Teapot," Anne uses the words "a look of freezing scorn" and "red as a beet" to describe how she looked at Josie Pye and how Josie reacted. Those phrases give us clear images of the exchange between the two girls.

Plot: Conflict and Resolution

The plot of a story is often based on conflict between characters. As the story progresses, that conflict usually grows and then is resolved at the story's end. In "Mattie and Angel," Mattie's conflict is with Angel. When Mattie is pushed down the stairs but decides not to get even, the conflict is resolved, at least for the time being.

Stereotypes

A stereotyped character is one who has all the qualities associated, often unjustly, with a group. For example, the wolf in "The Three Little Pigs" is characterized as ruthless and dangerous. "The Real Wolf" tries to show how this common stereotype is wrong.

Tone

The tone of a piece of writing is the author's attitude toward the subject. The tone of "Climbing Boys" is serious. The author gives the reader facts and details that show the hard lives of the young chimney sweeps. By contrast, the tone in "The Trial of the Big Bad Wolf" is light and humorous. The author uses exaggeration, stereotypical characters, and sarcasm to make us laugh at the antics of all involved in the trial.

Glossary

apprentice (def. 1)—
The boy at the right
is a printer's
apprentice.

dignity (def. 1)

Vocabulary from your selections

an tic i pate (an tis′ə pāt), look forward to; expect: *We are anticipating a good time at your party. v.,* **an tic i pat ed, an tic i pat ing.** —**an tic′i pa′tor,** *n.*

an tic i pa tion (an tis′ə pā′shən), act of anticipating; looking forward to; expectation: *In anticipation of a cold winter, they cut extra firewood. n.*

ap pren tice (ə pren′tis), **1** person learning a trade or art. In return for instruction the apprentice agrees to work for the employer a certain length of time with little or no pay. **2** beginner; learner. *n.*

bail iff (bā′lif), officer of a court of law who has charge of jurors and guards prisoners while they are in the courtroom. *n.*

civ i lized (siv′ə līzd), advanced in social customs, art, and science: *The ancient Greeks were a civilized people. adj.*

con fi den tial (kon′fə den′shəl), told or written as a secret: *a confidential report. adj.* —**con′fi den′tial ly,** *adv.*

con flict (kon′flikt), **1** a fight or struggle, especially a long one: *The UN General Assembly discussed the conflict in the Middle East.* **2** active opposition of persons or ideas; clash: *A conflict of opinion arose over the need for a new highway. n.*

de fend ant (di fen′dənt), person accused or sued in a court of law: *The defendant is charged with theft. n.*

dig ni ty (dig′nə tē), **1** proud and self-respecting character or manner; stateliness: *the dignity of a cathedral. The candidate maintained her dignity during the heated debate.* **2** degree of worth, honor, or importance: *A judge should maintain the dignity of his or her position.* **3** worth; nobleness: *Honest work has dignity. n., pl.* **dig ni ties.**

dis pute (dis pyüt′), **1** give reasons or facts for or against something; argue; debate; discuss: *Congress disputed over the need for new taxes.* **2** argument; debate: *There is a dispute over where to build the school.* **3** quarrel: *The children disputed over the only toy.* **4** a quarrel: *The dispute between the neighbors threatened their friendship.* 1,3 *v.,* **dis put ed, dis put ing;** 2,4 *n.*

dock et (dok′it), **1** list of lawsuits to be tried by a court. **2** any list of matters to be considered by some person or group. *n.*

do mes ti cate (də mes′tə kāt), **1** change from a wild to a tame or cultivated state: *People have domesticated many plants and animals.* **2** make fond of home and family life. *v.,* **do mes ti cat ed, do mes ti cat ing.**

ex ter mi nate (ek stèr′mə nāt), destroy completely: *This poison will exterminate rats. v.,* **ex ter mi nat ed, ex ter mi nat ing.**

flue (flü), tube, pipe, or other enclosed passage for smoke or hot air. A chimney often has several flues. *n.*

gas i fy (gas′ə fī), **-fied, -fy ing. 1** produce gas from or change into gas. **2** become gas. *v.* **—gas′i fi ca′tion,** *n.*

hav oc (hav′ək), very great destruction or injury: *Tornadoes can create widespread havoc. n.*
play havoc with, injure severely; ruin; destroy.

hu mil i ate (hyü mil′ē āt), lower the pride, dignity, or self-respect of; make ashamed: *We felt humiliated by our failure. They humiliated me by criticizing me in front of my friends. v.,* **hu mil i at ed, hu mil i at ing.**

lease (lēs), **1** the right to use property for a certain length of time by paying rent for it. **2** a written statement saying for how long a property is rented and how much money shall be paid for it. **3** length of time for which a lease is made. **4** give a lease on. **5** to rent: *We have leased an apartment for one year.* 1-3 *n.,* 4,5 *v.,* **leased, leas ing.**

a hat	oi oil
ā age	ou out
ä far	u cup
e let	u̇ put
ē equal	ü rule
ėr term	
i it	ch child
ī ice	ng long
o hot	sh she
ō open	th thin
ô order	ᴛʜ then
	zh measure

ə = {
a in about
e in taken
i in pencil
o in lemon
u in circus
}

havoc—havoc caused by an earthquake

mi nor i ty (mə nôr′ə tē *or* mī nôr′ə tē), **1** the smaller number or part; less than half: *A minority of the voters wanted a tax increase, but the majority defeated it.* **2** a group within a country, state, etc., that differs in race, religion, etc., from the larger part of the population. *n., pl.* **mi nor i ties.**

mis giv ing (mis giv′ing), a feeling of doubt, suspicion, or anxiety: *We started off through the storm with some misgivings. n.*

mis name (mis nām′), call by a wrong name. *v.,* **mis named, mis nam ing.**

pro hib it (prō hib′it), **1** forbid by law or authority: *Picking flowers in this park is prohibited.* **2** prevent: *Rainy weather and fog prohibited flying. v.*

proph e cy (prof′ə sē), **1** a telling what will happen; foretelling future events. **2** thing told about the future. *n., pl.* **proph e cies.**

pros e cu tion (pros′ə kyü′shən), side that starts action against another in a court of law. The prosecution makes certain charges against the defense. *n.*

rep u ta tion (rep′yə tā′shən), **1** what people think and say the character of a person or thing is; character in the opinion of others; name; repute: *This store has an excellent reputation for fair dealing. He has the reputation of being very bright.* **2** fame. *n.*

res er va tion (rez′ər vā′shən), land set aside by the government for a special purpose: *an Indian reservation. n.*

ri val (rī′vəl), person who wants and tries to get the same thing as another or who tries to equal or do better than another; competitor: *The two girls were rivals in sports and for the same class office. n.*

ru mor (rü′mər), **1** story or statement talked of as news without any proof that it is true: *The rumor spread that a new school would be built here.* **2** vague, general talk: *Rumor has it that the new girl went to school in France. n.*

shad ow (shad′ō), **1** shade made by some person, animal, or thing. **2** a little bit; small degree; slight suggestion: *They were innocent beyond the shadow of a doubt.* **3** person who follows another closely and secretly, as a detective. **4** a constant companion; follower. *n.*

shadow (def. 1)

soot (sùt *or* süt), a black substance in the smoke from burning coal, wood, oil, etc. Soot makes smoke dark and collects on the inside of chimneys. *n.*

suit (süt), **1** set of clothes to be worn together. A man's suit consists of a coat, pants, and sometimes a vest. A woman's suit consists of a coat and either a skirt or pants. **2** case in a court of law; application to a court for justice: *He started a suit to collect damages for his injuries.* **3** make suitable; make fit: *to suit the punishment to the crime.* **1,2** *n.,* **3** *v.*

tes ti mo ny (tes′tə mō′nē), statement used for evidence or proof: *A witness gave testimony that the defendant was at home all day Sunday. n., pl.* **tes ti mo nies.**

tres pass (tres′pəs), **1** go on somebody's property without any right: *We put up "No Trespassing" signs to keep hunters off our land.* **2** act or fact of trespassing. **3** do wrong; sin. **4** a wrong; a sin. **1,3** *v.,* **2,4** *n., pl.* **tres pass es.** —**tres′pass er,** *n.*

tu ber cu lo sis (tü bèr′kyə lō′sis *or* tyü bèr′ kyə lō′sis), an infectious disease affecting various tissues of the body, but most often the lungs. *n.*

vin dic tive (vin dik′tiv), **1** bearing a grudge; wanting revenge: *A vindictive person is unforgiving.* **2** showing a strong tendency toward revenge: *a vindictive act. adj.*

whiz *or* **whizz** (hwiz), **1** a humming or hissing sound. **2** move or rush with such a sound: *An arrow whizzed past his head.* **3** SLANG. a very clever person; expert. **1,3** *n., pl.* **whiz zes; 2** *v.,* **whizzed, whiz zing.**

wit ness (wit′nis), **1** person who saw something happen; spectator; eyewitness: *There were several witnesses to the accident.* **2** be a witness of; see: *He witnessed the accident.* **3** person who gives evidence or testifies under oath in a court of law. **4** evidence; testimony: *A person who gives false witness in court is guilty of perjury.* **1,3,4** *n., pl.* **wit ness es; 2** *v.* **bear witness,** be evidence; give evidence; testify: *The woman's fingerprints bore witness to her guilt. His blushes bore witness to his great embarrassment.*

a	hat	oi	oil
ā	age	ou	out
ä	far	u	cup
e	let	ù	put
ē	equal	ü	rule
èr	term		
i	it	ch	child
ī	ice	ng	long
o	hot	sh	she
ō	open	th	thin
ô	order	ᴛʜ	then
		zh	measure

$$ə = \begin{cases} \text{a in about} \\ \text{e in taken} \\ \text{i in pencil} \\ \text{o in lemon} \\ \text{u in circus} \end{cases}$$

suit (def. 1)

trespass (def. 1)

Acknowledgments

Text

Page 7: From *Circle of Gold* by Candy Dawson Boyd, pages 1-17. Copyright © 1984, by Candy Dawson Boyd. Reprinted by permission of Scholastic Inc.
Page 24: "Behind Circle of Gold: Changes and Choices" by Candy Dawson Boyd. Copyright © 1991 by Candy Dawson Boyd.
Page 30: "Peer Mediation" by Priscilla Prutzman and Judith M. Johnson. Copyright © 1991 by Children's Creative Response to Conflict Program, Nyack, NY.
Page 46: "Primer Lesson" from *Slabs of the Sunburnt West* by Carl Sandburg, copyright © 1922 by Harcourt Brace & Company and renewed 1950 by Carl Sandburg, reprinted by permission of the publisher.
Page 49: "A Tempest in the School Teapot" from *Anne of Green Gables* by L. M. Montgomery, 1908.
Page 65: "Climbing Boys" from *Chimney Sweeps: Yesterday and Today* by James Cross Giblin, illustrated by Margot Tomes. Text copyright © 1982 by James Cross Giblin. Illustrations copyright © 1982 by Margot Tomes. Reprinted by permission of HarperCollins *Publishers.*
Page 86: "Writing: An Adventure of Discovery" by James Cross Giblin. Copyright © 1991 by James Cross Giblin.
Page 90: "They Will Tear Up the Earth" from *Morning Star, Black Sun* by Brent Ashabranner. Text copyright © 1982 by Brent Ashabranner. Reprinted by permission of G. P. Putnam's Sons.
Page 101: "The Real Wolf" and "Wolves and Human History" from the book *Wolves* by Jane Rockwell, pages 1-2, 4, 5-6 and 8. Copyright © 1980 by Jane Rockwell. Reprinted by permission of the publisher, Franklin Watts, Inc.
Pages 110, 111: "The Grandmother" and "The Builders" from *Story Hour* by Sara Henderson Hay, copyright © 1982. Reprinted by permission of the University of Arkansas Press.
Page 112: "The Trial of the Big Bad Wolf" by Val R. Cheatham, from *Plays*, January 1981. Copyright © 1981 by Plays, Inc. Reprinted by permission.

Artists

Illustrations owned and copyrighted by the illustrator.
Cover: Guy Porfirio
Pages 1-3: Guy Porfirio
Pages 4, 6-29: Gwyn Stramler
Page 47: Tom Gieseke
Pages 48, 56-57, 59, 63: Chris Sheban
Pages 51, 54, 61: Johnston Clark
Pages 4, 64, 70 ,71, 75, 77, 79, 86, 88: Margot Tomes
Pages 90-99,127: Jon Conrad
Pages 112-126,127: David Rose

Photographs

Unless otherwise acknowledged, all photographs are the property of Scott Foresman.
Page 24: Courtesy of Candy Dawson Boyd
Page 25: Charles Gupton/Allstock
Pages 66-67: Ray Pfortner/Peter Arnold, Inc.
Page 83 top: Cooper-Hewitt Museum, the Smithsonian Institution
Page 87: Miriam Berkley
Page 103: Stock Imagery
Page 105: Jim Barandenburg/Allstock
Page 106: Robert Winslow
Page 108: Bauer/Allstock
Page 110: J.A. Kraulis/Masterfile
Page 111: H.D. Thoreau/Westlight
Page 132 top: The Granger Collection, New York
Page 132 bottom: Cecil Beaton, London, England
Page 133: Library of Congress
Page 134: Dan Morrill
Page 135 top: Blair Seitz
Page 135 bottom: Richard Hutchings/Photo Researchers

Glossary

The contents of the Glossary entries in this book have been adapted from *Scott, Foresman Intermediate Dictionary,* Copyright © 1988 by Scott, Foresman and Company, and *Scott, Foresman Advanced Dictionary,* Copyright © 1988 by Scott, Foresman and Company.